ECHOES FROM A WAR

For Julia and Sophie,
Simon and Jonathan

ECHOES FROM A WAR

Letters edited by
Graham Watson

The Book Guild Ltd
Sussex, England

First published in Great Britain in 2003 by
The Book Guild Ltd
25 High Street
Lewes, East Sussex
BN7 2LU

Typesetting in Baskerville by
IML Typographers, Birkenhead, Merseyside

Printed in Great Britain by
Bookcraft (Bath) Ltd, Avon

A catalogue record for this book is
available from The British Library

ISBN 1 85776 766 7

INTRODUCTION

The letters that follow are a selection from two hundred and twenty which passed between my sister, Diana (D), and I (G), during the Second World War while I served four years out of my six in the army in Egypt, Libya, Tunisia, Sicily, Italy, France, Belgium, Holland and Germany. During the same period, Diana endured the normal precarious existence which was the lot of the citizens of London.

The letters were divided almost equally between us – one hundred and eight from me and ninety-nine from Diana. Thirteen were never received, a pretty good record for the Army Post Office which involved, in my case, four separate theatres of war. All our letters were numbered so that we could determine which were missing. Perhaps the most surprising fact is that mine survived the distractions of the blitz and Diana's remained intact during my rather peripatetic war. More than fifty years have passed since they were written, during which the correspondence has lain unread in a drawer. The still unhealed wound of Diana's death from cancer in 1967 precluded me from wanting to disinter memories, largely forgotten, of a distant war.

However, circumstances arose when I was compelled to open the drawer and once again peruse the letters which it contained. They retained their immediacy for me and I consequently wondered whether they might have something to offer to those who, fortunately, will never have to endure the experiences that they relate. Of course, it is not only life before and during the war which has changed out of all recognition. For those of us born before or soon after the First World War, not only has our world undergone a material revolution, but the markers by which our lives were guided have almost disappeared. It is too late to expect those born after the Second World War to have any innate understanding of life before it, but there will never be a war similar to that between 1939 and 1945 and it may be of passing interest to discover how it was endured by at least two participants.

Because of the time lag between dispatch and receipt, which in the early days of the war was about six weeks, it was impossible to sustain a normal blow-by-blow corres-pondence, although both of us responded as best we could to the letters as they were received. Diana's letters were enormously longer and fuller than mine, averaging perhaps two thousand words. They included what she knew I longed for – every scrap of gossip or news affecting herself, the family, the war generally. She knew that I was avid for every bit of personal news, however trivial. The result is that a large proportion of these descriptions are of no conceivable interest to the present day reader, so I have cut them out and excluded the less interesting letters. My letters, on the other hand, suffered initially from the restraints of censorship which was lessened when I became commissioned half-way through the war.

Partly to fill a gap about campaigns in the desert in 1941–2 in which I was involved, but precluded from mentioning except in general terms, I have added three small extracts from my autobiography, *Book Society*, which was published some few years ago. Perhaps they may embellish the rather restrained accounts of the desert war as evidenced from my letters. For the same reason I have included my con-temporary account of life on a troop-ship which has never been published.

Diana's letters evoke strongly what it was like to live in

London during the blitz, with a variety of jobs, a husband and a family and house to look after. Many of her letters contain reflections on the war and the emotional tensions and expectations for the future which seem to me to throw light on the thoughts of someone living under great strain. From my side of the correspondence I hope I may have recaptured a little of the essence of service, initially as a gunner in the desert with the most distinguished professional artillery regiment in the army, and later as an officer in Sicily and Italy, before finally taking part in the landing in France on D-Day.

A little personal background is called for. When I came down from Cambridge in 1934 to work in a small family publishing business, I shared a flat with Diana, my senior by five years. We jointly had the spending of the princely sum of five hundred pounds, which enabled us to pursue something of a privileged and relatively social life, partly arising from friends in the book-trade, and mainly from the fact that Diana was a beautiful and much pursued woman. We shared an engaging circle of friends and, with a joint belief that war was imminent, made no attempt to look beyond the present. We watched, and wryly commented upon, the rather frequent romantic attachments in which, during those pre-war years, both of us were to a greater or lesser degree involved. And of course, during the five years in which we shared a flat in London, we developed a fond relationship for each other. No doubt that would have survived any changed circumstances which would inevitably have resulted from our subsequent respective marriages. But things were not to take their normal course.

In the modern world which has lost its innocence and whose principal yardsticks appear to be sex and money, it may be difficult for any individual to understand the terrible emotional pressures which had to be endured, personally and universally, by those whose loved ones were under the constant threat of annihilation. Searching for and discovering some rock, against which one's pent-up emotions could break, was a vital step in a situation almost impossible to bear but equally impossible to avoid. In my case, I came to find that rock in Diana, and although her own needs were to a large extent nourished by her husband and sons, she also responded to mine. The letters demonstrate a close relationship which arose from exceptional circumstances imposed on two people who had already developed a fondness for each other, different, of course, in intensity and different, of course, in expression. Doubtless these letters only differ in detail and personalities and circumstances from others written in the same period.

As to the cast and background information which it is necessary for the reader to possess, it is mercifully short as all the bit players have been removed. Those who remain answered to nicknames. My father (Pops) was a distinguished businessman based in Newcastle, who, throughout the war, was Divisional Food Officer for the North of England. A teetotaller, he was a man of deep religious principles which he had acquired during a strict Victorian upbringing, and which he had no difficulty in retaining, challenged as they were by the circumstances of the war. My mother (Mops) was a shy Northumbrian woman, who acted as a support group for her family. Diana's husband, Leslie, was too old for active service, but he spent the war in London, in the Grenadier Guards. He and his son, who was born in 1942, both acquired the designation 'Mole', arising from the imagined need to burrow underground to avoid the bombing. My sister Hazel (Magin) joined the Land Army on the outbreak of war and subsequently wrote a funny book about it, *Green Hands*. Later, she transferred to the ATS (Auxiliary Transport Service). Peter was a large and ancient Pekinese who controlled the family according to his immediate needs. Mrs Bagnall, who also has an important part in these pages, was a pig, acquired by the rude and licentious soldiery. She was much loved and she survived until it was agreed that the fattening up process was sufficient to meet our needs. My designation (Wogger) was foisted on me as being a 'Western Oriental Gentleman'.

Graham Watson

London, SW1

March 17th, 1941

Graham – my darling,

After a lot of thought and hesitation I am writing to you because sometimes it is easier to put down on paper thoughts which are not easy to express, rather than to try and say them. If I do it badly, please believe it is only because I love you that I am trying to do it, and forgive me.

Do you remember when we talked one night together at Whitewell[1] and I told you I longed to have something outside myself to give me courage and faith during all the months to come when we might be faced with every sort of dread and fear? I haven't found a faith yet but because I think you are searching too I thought perhaps we could help each other so that when the time comes for us to face whatever lies before us we can know that we are not alone. I think we are both willing to believe in a God, or goodness, but are unable to find any contact or conviction that it is possible. Perhaps our approach is wrong – perhaps prayer is not a question of petition and response but a daily avowal that we believe in goodness. The response may come almost unknown to ourselves. Since I came to the conclusion at the beginning of the year that I couldn't depend on myself alone for strength, that it was essential to find something more than human to sustain me, almost unawares my fear has gone. When I came back to London I found I was ready to face whatever was to come, not tensely and afraid, but calmly assured that strength would be given me.

Perhaps I am wrong and my new found serenity will ooze

_____
[1] The family home

1

away from me, but I don't believe so. I don't know why this has happened but I like to think there is a personal God who is loving and understanding even to those of us who can't approach him, who answers prayers which are never spoken or even very consciously formed. You may think this is superstitious nonsense but my belief is certain, no matter how illogical or false, and I believe that if I go step-by-step I will find strength to bear whatever comes as I go along. It doesn't seem to me to be important what we believe in so long as we know there is something outside ourselves greater than ourselves which will be there to turn to in our need.

I wondered if it would help us both while you are away if each night we know that we were both thinking and trying to pray for each other. Perhaps if we knew that we shared the same need and were approaching together the unknown humbly and uncertainly we might be given not only courage for our present need but the beginning of a permanent and certain faith. I wish I could give you something real that was worth having. I shall have failed you so dreadfully if you leave with only the memory of a few good times and nothing more. That is why I am risking seeming presumptuous and silly. It hurts me to think that I can be so useless.

I want to tell you, too, how very deeply and proudly I admire your courage and respect you for the way you have chosen deliberately a difficult road and are sticking it so uncomplainingly. I am so very proud of you, darling, and my belief in you and all that you do, both now and in the future, is unfaltering.

I can never tell you how at times you have made life entirely worth living nor thank you for it. When you go, part of me will go with you, but I will try to match my courage with yours, happy in the certainty that soon you will be back again with all the happiness of peace to look forward to. I won't worry because I shall still feel very close to you no matter how far away you are, and I will do what I can to help Mummy and Daddy to bear your absence.

I shall miss you more horribly than I can bear to admit but I shall pray that it won't be for long. You will be in my thoughts every day.

D

✍

Woolwich

March 19th, 1941

Very darling D,

I was deeply moved by your letter. Nowadays while we are all living on this precarious razor-edge of life, emotions like love, faith and loyalty, while always of priceless value, now seem to take on an even heightened intensity. Paradoxically, if one is not to become an emotional wreck, they have to be fairly suppressed. One cannot, now, afford the luxury of grief because it is so much more intensely felt. I do, however, want to say that you have made my life – particularly these last few months – an easily bearable burden. The courage you have shown is an inspiration that nonetheless makes me feel intensely humble. The faith and trust you (and all the family) put in me gives me aspirations that I must never betray. I cannot even begin to hint at the debt I will ever owe you and the enrichment that you have brought me.

I have always believed that fundamentally – and making allowances for the differences in sex – we are both temperamentally the same. It came as a great joy, therefore, but not as a surprise, to find that with your feminine intuition you had been able to crystallize thoughts that I had dimly been conscious of in my mind for some months. As you have

3

long known ever since I joined the army I have felt that there was a fore-ordained course that my life in it would follow. I have never had any cause to doubt this. I have always believed that I may suffer untold discomforts, fears and horrors but that finally, having survived it all, I would come out of it enriched and deepened – as steel is tempered by fire. I told this to Father. 'My dear boy,' he said, 'if you believe there is a pattern to your life you have gone a long way along the road to believing there is a God – or some agency that is responsible for that pattern.' And I am, I believe, slowly beginning to believe, he is, of course, right. Since I joined the army I have always believed that courage to take it was one of the great virtues which we had to possess. I don't know how much I possess it but I do know that when I have been faced with a test such as I never believed I could have stomached I have so far always found some hidden resource on which I can draw. I don't yet know what that faith is based on but I am daily beginning to believe it's not just myself. I have doubted, asked for strength and have been given it. I'm beginning to believe I always will be given it, so long as my motives in asking are honest to myself. Would Father call this prayer? I suspect he would.

This world is going through a pretty big shaking up. Either the evil in men will triumph or the good. Neither you nor I believe it will be the evil. No-one will ever be quite the same again for things which you and I are looking for and daily beginning to realise are, of course, the common experience of every one of us – which in itself is rather a comfort. No, I believe, we will all be finer people for what we are going through.

I think that your idea of thinking of each other and trying to help each other each night is a lovely one – tho' I don't promise only to think of you at night. But even without this help – and it will be a tremendous help to me – you will be all right. For even if you don't know why or what it is you've got your faith – as I think I have – and it will never let you down. You will often be frightened, often in despair, often sickened in the days to come but you cannot fail to be true to your ideals and yourself. Because then it wouldn't be you. And when it's all over and we take up the strings of life again, I think we'll be more worthwhile people for it.

I shall try not to worry about you, darling D, as I hope you will try not to worry about me. And I shall be leaving you in good keeping, the keeping of the good, wise, kindly rock that is L.H. Gault, Esq.

I don't think I shall be away long – even a year is not much in terms of our life still ahead of us – and I shall dream daily of the day we shall meet again. And don't, don't doubt yourself – you'll never let yourself down.

This letter, D, must be my good-bye – or rather au revoir – to you. Neither of us could bear to say good-bye properly.

May God keep you safe.

G

&

Whitton Grange[1],
Rothbury,
Northumberland

March 29th, 1941

Graham, darling,

Writing to you seems as momentous and formidable as talking down 'Mother England's' ear-trumpet: either every detail, even the most trivial and absurd, is important or

---

[1] The family country house

5

nothing seems sufficiently so to send across so many perilous miles.

I can only make wild guesses as to where you are and the sort of people you are with, whereas every detail of these surroundings is as familiar and unchanged as a photograph album. The chairs with the rather awful chintzes (one distinctly marked by your lurid Savoy hair-oil), Mops on one side of the fire reading and every other moment stopping to chat or turn on the wireless, Hazel in a peculiar assortment of riding clothes sprawled in another chair, Peter[1] gumfling away to himself in a corner. There is a smudge of damp on the wall near the fire-place, which Mops tried to improve with a different coloured paint, otherwise it is all so familiar to you that you know every word already.

I came up on Friday, motoring from Newcastle with Pops and his aged crony (a rather sweet little man like dry fizzy ginger ale). We arrived in a snow storm and had the usual business of carrying in our own luggage. It won't surprise you to know that we had fish for supper but no cheese, so my insides clanged together with hunger and Mops was rather canny with the coal so as to impress the 'aged crony' that rationing was a serious business. I haven't felt so cold or hungry since I was at Roedean!

The days have been habitually idle. After-lunch stupors until tea-time, gentle walks across the moors punctuated by waits for Peter. Yesterday the snow vanished and spring seemed suddenly to be there. Long shadows drifted over the hills and the sky was empty except for a lark singing high up above us – it all seemed so serene and eternal.

Mummy is in very good form and is being very wise and philosophical about you going away. The fact that you have gone makes her feel that the war is nearer to finishing and that you will be home again and the world will be at peace

---

[1] Peter, the family Pekinese

6

quite soon. Pops also is in good spirits as his faith in the future is unshakeable.

Your letter was, and is, a great joy to me. It helped me enormously to bear your going. After I spoke to you on the telephone before you sailed I felt as though a part of me had been amputated but I gradually felt we were very near to each other no matter what distance separated us and then, when every corner of the flat and of London spoke to me of you, it was nice and no longer hurt.

Before leaving London, I was making strenuous attempts to organise (or help to organise) our fire-watching. I have never quite realised before the stubborn resistance of the great British Public, of all classes. I became rather bad-tempered after several unsuccessful efforts to enlist the interest of some of our new neighbours and my last attempt happened to be a one-armed woman who was most offensive. Obviously active in any respect in which she was interested, she shook her stump and claimed immunity on those grounds. Rather savagely I replied that I thought we would be lucky if at the end of the war anyone was left with arms, legs or teeth. Since then the spirit of neighbourliness is a little dimmed.

I wonder if you are languishing in lovely, radiant sunshine. If your prognostications are justified you will not, at any rate, be languishing! I hope you have somebody there with whom you can talk and giggle over the same things. Your first letter will be enormously exciting even if every other line is black with censoring. I expect a lot of my letters will never reach you so I will number them and you can tell if any fail to arrive. Do let me know if it is possible to send you anything, books, papers, food or anything?

Nothing much has happened in London since you left. No bombs. Doing very little and seeing very few people. I will try to scavenge some news for my next letter as I am afraid this is a very dull one. I have rambled on because it is fun to talk to

7

you again. I am trying to be brave and patient like you and I turn to your letter often for strength and comfort. It will be easier to bear your absence if I could feel that your conditions were not too uncongenial and that you were tolerably happy.

I will finish this off now and hope that it will reach you somewhere. Bless you, darling.

D

ॐॐ

Gunner G.A. Watson 979135
2nd Echelon, G.H.Q.
Army P.O. 890

April 21st, 1941

Very darling D,[1]

I haven't written to you previously because you will have had my news and 'news' is seldom worth repeating. As to my feelings I was, and am, doubtful as to the value of writing of reactions to a situation which will be finished with long before the letter can be delivered. This letter, therefore, will be no letter but the result of the random vagaries of my pen. Perhaps it will not prove worth writing but I feel the wish to communicate with you and this is the best way I can do it.

I have read and re-read your letter to me. It has cheered me up when I was depressed and lonely, encouraged me when I felt doubt and fear, given me hope in a future when I have sometimes doubted whether there will ever be one. You

---

[1] This letter was written on a troop-ship

are never, of course, far from my thoughts but I feel very close to you most at the time of our nightly pact. As I lie in bed I often think that I can hear you standing by encouraging me. I like to think that you feel my own love and blessings nightly yourself. Will you try and go further, D? There isn't, of course, any doubt about telepathy. No two people should be so easily able to get in touch with each other as we two. Will you send me a message regarding your safety each night? I will do the same. I shall never be able to tell you what you have meant to me – particularly during these past months. And now I sail into an unknown and by all accounts terrifying future with confidence and assurance. For I see it as the largest and possibly the last obstacle that I have to surmount to justify myself and, with the belief of those who love me, I trust I shall not fail them. You, too, D, face the same hour of destiny in far-away London. You cannot fail, bless you. Do you remember in *Gone With The Wind* that passage about Gotterdammerung: the Twilight of the Gods? How history boringly repeats itself. Perhaps each generation of people must go along the same narrow circumscribed lesson life has to teach. It's as if someone has apparently decided to put the world through a crammer! One fact which I find encouraging is that no experience can be altogether unendurable which is the lot of so many millions.

My general state of mind remains in the incredible groove of indifference, of emotional stability that it has been in ever since I joined the army. I still worry a little when I read of air-raids on London but somehow I feel you will be safe. I sometimes feel depressed at the endless vista of war and disturbances that seems to stretch ahead of us (there seems so little chance that we shall even recognise in the future a life which is even a passing likeness to the one we knew). Mostly I spend my time either not thinking at all, being intensely bored, or fuming in a perfectly detached way at the totally unbelievable futility of the army. I use the world 'unbelievably' advisedly. I very much doubt if you would believe me if I were allowed – which I'm not – to tell you some of it. Even this, however, doesn't worry me personally. I pursue my way with as much equanimity as possible. It's very curious this emotional sterility. I wonder whether I will get back my power to feel when I return to civil life. In connection with this I wonder why the last war was able to produce so many good poets. For *they* must have felt things. Perhaps the difference is that they were fighting for an ideal – that they were going to better the world. Whereas we are fighting for self-preservation and the pretty certain knowledge that the world will be even more disagreeable. Then, too, we've had twenty years of disillusionment when we looked out on trickery in high places and indifference in low; on the worship of false gods and the iconoclasm of true ones; on the reversal of values and the cheapening of sentiment so that sincerity became a reason for sniggering, loyalty a cause of abuse and true emotions a creator of embarrassed silence. Thank God, however, we are sufficiently honest to be able to see this war as it is – a dirty business – and not attempt to glorify it with cheap heroics.

I must put this letter aside for the time. I am getting so hot writing it below decks I cannot go on in comfort. I must go upstairs and look at the moon – not a bomber's moon here, no thanks to Hitler – and the stars winking out of their velvet and the phosphorescent waves creaming their way along the ship. I shall continue this scribble another day. For tonight, my dearest love and blessing. I shall talk to you again at ten o'clock. God keep you safe.

April 22nd

With no present, and no future, my thoughts are largely dwelling in the past – and what a good past it was! God knows

I have been blest in my twenty-eight years of life. The view up Ullswater before dropping down the hill into How Town[2]; La Conga at the Embassy[3]; the long climb over a Scottish hill till one sees the loch glistening, and full of trout, in the distance; Whitton baking in the sun of an August afternoon; Toy Town Tavern and the Mohawk trail[4]; white tie and gardenias at the Dorchester; the Avon lazing by Salisbury Cathedral; wisteria at Portofino; the silken motion of a punt on the Cam; roulette at Arcachon; the Sunday Times crossword and the Phillipses on a weekend trip; Neville at St Abbs Head;[5] the lights going down in a London theatre; Carrington House and all six years of it[6]; the Alwinton valley golden in the evening sun and Sugar Sands white in a morning one; Paternoster Row[7]; the Simonside Hills[8]; these and thousands of other equally good memories provide a storehouse which would make any man rich. Some of them and others, perhaps equally good, will come again.

The news continues bad. My belief in an ultimate victory is largely now an article of faith. If there is any moral force operating it should be certain. If one were to rely on unvarnished facts the outcome would be much more doubtful. Still I suppose the facts in possession of any of us are too small to allow us to judge the whole affair impartially. In any event there is nothing I can do about it, so I suppose it would be foolish to worry about what cannot be altered. Certain it is that we are paying a terrible price for our ineptitude in recent years. The mistake that one is so apt to make of

[2] In the Lake District
[3] A popular London nightclub of the period
[4] An American trail in New England
[5] The Phillipses and Neville were old family friends; St Abbs Head is a promontory near Berwick
[6] Carrington House in Shepherds Market was our London flat
[7] Pasternoster Row was the address of my office
[8] Simonside is the name of the moors near Whitton Grange

course, is thinking that all the problems and inefficiency are on our side. The Germans, no doubt, have their own worries.

I am reading with considerable pleasure Oscar Wilde's collected works. At the moment I am busy with *Picture of Dorian Gray*. What a joy it is with its paradoxical wit and wisdom. E.g. 'nowadays most people die of a sort of creeping common sense and discover when it is too late that the only things one never regrets are one's mistakes.' Or 'One of those middle-aged mediocrities who have no enemies but are thoroughly disliked by their friends.' Or '... with one of those characteristic British faces, that once seen are never remembered.' The whole book is like that. Coward has never equalled it. I enjoyed very greatly, too, *The Pickwick Papers*. It is curious to see how closely some of Wodehouse's humour is correlated to Dickens. I never noticed it before when I read the book. Indeed, I didn't think it so funny the first time. Here is my reading since I have been on board. *Theatre* – Somerset Maugham. A good novel but a bad Maugham. How Lilian Braithwaite[9] must have hated it! Was it her? *Crime and Punishment* by Dostoievsky. Grand and sombre, stylistically atrocious. *Robin Linnet* by E.F. Benson. Pleasant and unimportant and a good deal too much last war for me. *Canon In Residence* by V.L. Whitechurch, gone into about 15 editions since 1906 and I can't think why. *National Velvet* by Enid Bagnold, a joyous novel. Don't miss it. *Literary Lapses* by Stephen Leacock. Dated since I read them last. *Pickwick Papers*, see above. My choice of reading is circumscribed by what I brought on board and what limited choice they have on sale at the Naafi.[10]

---

[9] A well-known West End actress
[10] Navy Army Air Force Institute

April 24th

It is very curious how the importance one attaches to various things is completely altered comparing this primitive existence with normal life. The food, for example, on this boat is absolutely wretched – it is either bad (through the heat) and, therefore, uneatable or so unappetising as to be uneatable (greasy mutton stews in the tropics!). Now normally I don't care a damn if the food is bad. If it is either one gets it improved or uses supplementary supplies to satisfy one's hunger. But here one is absolutely foxed as there are no supplementary supplies! It says a great deal for the nutritive values of bread. Actually, of course, no army meals can ever be regarded as a pleasure – food is simply a necessity so that the fact one finds the food now additionally unpleasant does not matter so long as we get enough of something to eat – which seems to be the case. It does, of course, intensely irritate me when I think how good it could be – as it is on some of the other boats on the convoy. After all, it is Cunard White Star catering and they should do well. Do you remember those meals we had on the *Berengaria*[11] under the aegis of the maître d'hôtel from the Berkeley, that *crêpe suzette*! I am, of course, the first to agree that this is hardly a fair comparison! But as a gourmet and a gourmand of no years' standing you will hardly doubt my words on the subject. Meanwhile, darling D, I think of that last dinner I never ate but which will be my first on landing: Borscht (with much whipped cream); grilled salmon, new potatoes and peas; raspberry fool. Simple, but very good! I will sleep on that, I think. Good-night, sleep well.

---

[11] A transatlantic liner on which we travelled to America

April 28th

I can foresee that any day now may prove to be the last instalment of this letter. The heat is in the region of the 100s in the shade and we are told will go up to the 120s before we are finished. As a result my hand moves stickily over clammy paper and life is a little too hot to be pleasant. I've been playing a good deal of chess lately. This is again something of a reversal to my schooldays as I have not played since then, except those two or three games with Leslie. I'm packing up now. It's getting too uncomfortable. I'll try and write later today!

P.M. I'll continue this now in the cool of the evening – a mere 90 or so! However, I'm ensconced under one of the ship ventilators and if I pick my hand off the paper each time I want to move it I should be able to manage.

I was thinking today what very good days those were when I was at Woolwich before leaving. Those nights and weekends we spent together are memories of a happiness which I never expected to have when actively involved in the army. What good meals we had, too. You know, D, you and I have had some crashingly good times together in the last few years. How tremendously happy I am that you've got Leslie to look after you now. I don't think I shall ever forget turning up at your flat at 2 a.m. on leave and telling a very sleepy subaltern that I'd had some of his whisky. And then for 20 minutes while I talked to you there was the muttered monotone continuously in the background: 'Whisky! What whisky! There's no whisky in the house. At least not that I know of.' It was a sort of Pooh Bear hum. He went on growling away till he was allowed back to bizer.[12] When I phoned from

---

[12] bed

14

Woolwich I didn't feel up to speaking to anybody but you. I'm sorry to have left that way, D, but it was the best way, you know. We'd both said our real good-byes a dozen times in our hearts.

Incidentally, I've just read this letter through and I'm not sure it doesn't give the impression of being written in rather a minor key. If so I've given you the wrong impression. Nobody could pretend they're enjoying this trip. Nobody could pretend they are looking forward to anything but the end of it all, as being the only moment worth looking forward to. On the other hand it is a really terrific experience that I would be sorry to miss. And I'm certainly not unhappy – just bovinely unfeeling.

We had a debate yesterday on 'marriage maketh man'. I confined myself to making a dirty crack on the subject of life on board. Neither then nor at the voluntary lectures earlier on in the voyage that were given, did I speak. I would have gladly given a lecture on some subject or other but I see no reason why I should use what qualifications I possess in helping the army to fill up time when they refuse to utilize the same qualifications for more useful purposes. Sour grapes, perhaps, but then the army does make me behave like a child. As their whole training is designed to that end they should be happy. Actually, at the debate I wanted to ask who the hell wants to be a man anyhow? When I joined the army I was told it would make a man of me – and look at me – the result of twelve months handiwork – an inefficient scullery maid-cum-lavatory attendant! Well, my love, I've talked enough rubbish for today. So good-night and God bless you and keep you safe.

May 1st

I must end this now. We land – or hope to! – in a day or two and this has to be censored in the interval. This six weeks trip

15

completes another paragraph in my hand-book of army life. You will have gathered – perhaps I have emphasised too *ad nauseam* – that it has not been a perfect pleasure cruise. But I swear I would not have missed a second of it for anything. I wish no more of the future than that I should be able to say the same of it.

Since I last wrote to you nothing to report has happened. It has got gradually hotter. We are still saved the bane of flies and things which will, I suppose, put the final touch to the discomfort of heat on shore.

We have also had another admirable concert at which two agreeable songs were sung which were composed on board by a gunner in memory of the voyage. I imagine they will both be published so think of me if you hear them – called *Fair Wind* and *Chins Up* – loathsome title. There is certainly no doubt that the officers who have been in charge of our draft have been a great deal more go-ahead on behalf of our amusement and comfort than those of any other draft. I expect that most of their efforts have as usual been stifled by those at the top.

Well, darling D, I close this with reluctance. It has been my companion for more than ten days and has proved a substitute – such a feeble one – to yourself. Still I have grown fond of it and I hand it to the care of the Army Post Office with reluctance. I hope it may reach you.

I long to hear from you. As I do not need to repeat you are always in my thoughts and very close to me. May God keep you very safe and give you his blessings. Meanwhile I have no doubt that it won't be long before we meet again. Till that wonderful moment I am your always devoted,

G

The following description of life on board the troop-ship was written in the desert as part of a projected, but never completed, book on life in the army. It should be read in conjunction with the letter dated 21 April 1941, which was subject to censorship.

Pasteurisation, 1941

We left Gourock on March 25 on His Majesty's troop-ship *Pasteur*, which was to be our home through cold, hot and stormy weather for seven long and weary weeks.

I am going to describe the *Pasteur* and our life on board in some detail because the conditions we endured were reproduced almost identically on all other troop-ships sailing to the Middle East. They represent a triumph of disorganisation and discomfort which surprised even those with long army experience. Whether there were any mutinies on board a troop-ship during the war I do not know. If there were not it can only be attributed to the long-suffering tolerance of the British soldier.

The *Pasteur* was a French luxury liner of 30,000 tons. She had been built at the time war was declared and had never, so far as I am aware, been in regular service on a passenger run. When France surrendered she was lying in a Canadian port and, after an attempt to scuttle her by part of her French crew, we took her over.

She was a beautifully appointed, roomy, luxurious ship with a large amount of deck-space, numerous spacious public rooms, a swimming bath and cabins each with their own bathroom. This was her condition before she was refitted as a troop-ship. In refitting her A, B, C and D decks, the first-class quarters, were left practically untouched and were taken over by the officers and, in our case, some few V.A.D. nurses who were travelling with us. A small section of this part of the boat was reserved for the use of warrant officers and sergeants. The swimming pool was boarded over to serve as a store-house and a few troop bunks were erected in a boarded off section on A and B decks. In effect, therefore, the officers' quarters were the normal first-class passengers' quarters, little altered. E and F decks, the second- and third-class passengers' sections, were, on the other hand, almost completely gutted. The cabins had all been removed and in their place had been fitted 'mess-decks'. Our mess-deck was about thirty-five feet long by about twelve feet across, by eight feet high. It contained six long, narrow tables, twelve hard, narrow bunks, a few small luggage racks on the ceiling, one small salt-water wash-basin for all washing up which was shared by another mess-deck, who had none themselves, and a fresh-water tap and a dip basin. The tap, however, provided warm brown water and was rightly put out of bounds at once so that we had to descend to another deck to get drinking water. This was all the furniture. In this space one hundred and four men were supposed to eat and sixty-eight men sleep. It may be doubted whether this latter feat was possible. In order that it could be accomplished hammocks were suspended from the ceiling, so close together as to be touching one another, and the remainder slept on the floor and the tables. Such arrangements were, it is obvious, hardly likely to encourage good health. The authorities, however, decided to make doubly sure of sickness. All ventilation was, of course, artificial. To offset any cold air that came in through the blowers, a series of uncovered hot-water pipes ran along the walls. Furthermore the cook-house was immediately above our heads on the deck above and the smell of cooking used to waft down the open staircase that was our only exit and entrance. As a final spirited gesture the bulkhead doors were all shut so that there was no through ventilation round the ship.

I have written of conditions as they prevailed on our mess-deck. They could be almost identically duplicated on all of them. Some mess-decks may have been bigger: then they had more men in them. Others may have been a slightly different shape according to the position on the ship. Such, however, were the living conditions for nearly four thousand men on a seven week voyage through the tropics. The comparison with the cabins and ballrooms inhabited by the two or three hundred officers is not an agreeable one.

The comparison, if anything, becomes even more marked when the question of public rooms is considered. The officers, as I have mentioned, had the run of the normal first-class lounge, dining room, writing room, etc. (The smoking room was reserved for the warrant officers and sergeants.) The four thousand lost souls had two canteens at their disposal. One in the bows of the ship was the size of a billiard room. At its three windows you could buy cigarettes, tea, lemonade, chocolate, biscuits, fruit and toilet necessities. The second canteen, in the stern of the ship was about half the size of a billiard room. In it you could buy tea and biscuits, an adulterated and almost undrinkable form of beer, and cigarettes. There was, of course, no room to sit down in either of the canteens.

But such an inconvenience was trifling compared to that of getting served. Most men wished to help out the appalling food by daily purchases of fruit and chocolate. It was only possible, however, to get these commodities at the foreward canteen – and only at two windows there, the third being reserved for tea. In addition, the canteen was only open at certain prescribed hours. The result is not difficult to forecast. It involved waiting in a queue for anything between an hour and two hours and a half, according to your luck.

Such conditions, of course, were not to be tolerated, and even the authorities were at last stirred to action. Not, as we had optimistically expected, by giving us the use of their lounge, but by introducing a system of bulk-buying by sections. This system had to be modified, for some reason, to bulk-buying of cigarettes and chocolate only. All other articles had to be bought as before at the canteen. When we got into hot weather nobody wanted chocolate, everybody wanted fruit. The queue remained much as it always had been.

The day we left the Clyde saw the beginning of the great invasion of deck space. The British soldier will tolerate a great deal but beyond a certain point he is immoveable. When this point is reached without any undue fuss he takes for himself what he considers to be his minimum due. This point was reached when we got into the Atlantic. There was an unpleasant swell and very soon people started to be sick. They had nowhere else to be sick except on the mess-deck where we were endeavouring to eat our meals. Seeing them, not unnaturally, made others ill. Soon four-fifths of the boat was affected, and there was nowhere for them to lie down, as no hammocks were allowed to be slung till 8.30 in the evening. There was only one solution. They invaded the decks. And there they stayed for the rest of the voyage, alleviating considerably the overcrowding downstairs.

It is impossible to give an adequate picture of the *Pasteur* on those first few days after sailing. But to try and give some idea I must digress with another aspect of that ship, the sanitary arrangements. Set into the bows and the stern of the boat were two corrugated iron structures and on the top deck there was a further space set aside. These were the only three lavatories on board for the use of the troops. The bow ones which were nearest to my mess-deck were in almost Stygian darkness. They were flushed on the elementary system of a continuous flow of sea-water down a pipe. When the pipe got blocked or the boat was pitching, the whole issue used to flood onto the floor. Not exactly conditions designed to improve the state of anyone who was sea-sick.

There were three sets of enamel, hand wash-basins on board, with about twenty basins in each set. The water was turned on between 5 and 7 a.m. (reveille was only at 6 a.m.), 11 a.m. and 12 p.m., and 6 to 8 p.m. There were about forty showers in all, and no bathrooms. There was no laundry and washing clothes in the circumstances was next to impossible. We had one change of clothes and were passing through weather that made us almost wringing wet with sweat. The smell on that boat was like an Eastern ghetto. Such were the sanitary arrangements for, I repeat, almost four thousand men. Not, I would suggest again, a pleasant comparison with the officers' cabins with a bathroom each.

In parentheses here I would like to mention how we were told on parade by our major: 'I know you can't buy razor blades at the canteen. I know the water is only on between 5 and 7 in the mornings, but I'm not going to have you come on parade unshaven. Shaving the night before won't do.'

Perhaps it would be wiser to leave to the imagination the effects of our living quarters, combined with such sanitary facilities, on a boat-load of sea-sick men. It was not a pleasant experience.

There is one more important question with which I must deal before going on to discuss life on board. This concerns food. Catering on board should, in my view, have presented no difficulties. The authorities knew exactly the number they had to feed, for how long and under what conditions. They managed to excel themselves with a lack of imagination typical of the whole organisation. It must be remembered that after the first two or three days we were in tropical heat the whole time.

For breakfast we had porridge, fish, eggs or something similar with tea or coffee. For lunch hot, thick soup and stew alternating with meat, beans and potatoes. For tea stew or bully beef and semi-cold potatoes left from lunch, with steamed pudding or tapioca. This was the almost unvarying diet although occasionally the changes were rung by sub-

21

stituting turnip for beans and sago for tapioca. Such a diet was totally unsuitable for very hot weather. In addition, the food was frequently bad, fish, eggs and meat particularly so, later even the bread. Finally, the last meal of the day was served at five o'clock, which meant going for fourteen hours before the next.

After leaving Freetown, like many others I lived almost exclusively on fruit which I bought at the canteen, only descending to meals to get some bread or a plate of soup. Once more I must make a comparison between our conditions and those of the officers. We saw their menus and their meals were almost as extensive as one is accustomed to find on such boats on their normal service. Fruit and cold collations rightly predominated. Fruit and cold collations figured in our menus only by their total absence.

Such were the conditions under which we lived for seven weeks. When we reached Port Suez we were low spirited and in poor physical condition. I do not think it is surprising. Faced by the embarkation authorities with conditions of such grotesque overcrowding there was little that the ship's officers travelling with us could do in the way of providing us with training or recreational programmes. It was a sufficiently difficult problem finding deck space in which all the troops could parade at one time, even though they stood in four ranks shoulder to shoulder. In this respect our draft fared better, I believe, than most of the others. Our major was alive to the danger of leaving more time than could be helped on the hands of men living under such conditions. Each day he made an attempt to arrange something which would help to pass the time. Even so, it was little enough that he could do.

The day started with reveille at six o'clock. Breakfast followed at seven. During this period the decks were washed down and, remaining wet for some considerable time after, further complicated the question of sitting down. Perhaps here would be a good moment to digress concerning this superficially small, but in fact fundamentally important problem, which was in addition to others we had to solve. None other than this question of sitting down! There were, of course, no chairs of any sort on deck. But, decks being extremely hard, only the most luxuriously upholstered posteriors could endure being sat upon for long without feeling acute discomfort. As an alternative, but equally hard seat, there was all the way around the ship, enclosed in a wooden box, the degausing (anti-magnetic mine) apparatus. This was equally hard but had the merit of being raised a few inches from the deck. The partial solution of our difficulties was found to be to lie on our life-belts which we always carried with us. Those made of cork were almost as uncomfortable as the deck. Those made of stuffing were a little better. As the latter were only issued to a small proportion of the whole, they became the most sought-after article of equipment on board. If one took one's eye off them for a second they were gone. I am glad to say I kept mine throughout the voyage. But to do so, my vigilance was ceaseless and untiring.

We found to our sorrow that there was no comfortable solution to the problem. And as we spent the greater part of the day in this form of suspended animation, we had to adopt a technique of altering the sitting position with that of a more recumbent posture and back again. But lying down was, in fact, little better than sitting. Though one could cushion one's head on the degausing apparatus, the rest of one's body was lying among all the grimy rubbish that somehow seemed always to litter a deck that was constantly being swept. A further difficulty was the fact that there was not sufficient room for more than a few to lie down together at any one time.

After we had breakfast, time was our own till ten o'clock, when we all paraded on deck for the Captain's ship inspection. As, however, the water was turned off at seven, we were unable to spend these three hours in cleaning ourselves up for the day. The morning parade lasted till about 11.30, and during it we had the ship's news read to us. Afterwards on most days we were given a short lecture on some topic of general interest. Some of the lectures were excellent. Others were given by officers who will, I trust, not endeavour to repeat the experiment when they return to civilian life. They are unlikely to find another audience so acquiescent. But then audiences in civil life have no threat of a court-martial hanging above their heads. What a paradise the army is for a bore!

At 12 we had lunch and paraded again at two o'clock. The afternoon parade was a short one and was usually concerned with such matters as pay, medical inspections and the like. Then, with tea at five o'clock, we were free till lights out at 9.30. In addition to this programme, we had occasional guards, fatigues and look-out duties to perform. But these were all of a relatively easy variety and only came our way occasionally.

It will be seen, therefore, that we had a large amount of time to ourselves. How did we fill it in? Well, not by physical exercise. In this connection, the lack of space again proved an insuperable difficulty. We were supposed to have two periods of physical training a week, each lasting for thirty minutes. In fact I myself, for one reason or another, had four periods during the whole voyage. This was a fairly typical experience. This was the total amount of exercise I had during seven weeks, with the exception of two route marches in Cape Town. It is true that half-hearted attempts were made to organise boxing and tug-of-war tournaments. But these only affected a very small proportion of the whole. This lack of exercise, was, I am sure, largely responsible for our steadily deteriorating state of health as the voyage wore on.

Books inevitably proved our main solace and most people

spent the greater part of the day in either reading or sleeping. Even those who had never previously read a book – and there were many – could be seen studiously absorbing the improbable adventures of the Texan Ranger and his colleagues. As the voyage wore on, it became increasingly difficult to borrow books. As a result, people were glad to read anything they could lay their hands on. I got a certain amount of sardonic satisfaction from lending out my own slender stock of books and watching their readers wade, with set and determined face, through them. *Pride and Prejudice* and *Wuthering Heights*, I always told the prospective borrower, were 'the book of the film, you know', *Crime and Punishment* was accepted with alacrity as 'a murder story'. *Picture of Dorian Gray* was by 'that man who was jugged for sodomy and had one of his plays banned'. *Vanity Fair* was 'about an attractive tart'. And *Pickwick Papers* was 'a funny book'. I had no hesitation about thus sugaring the pill of good literature. When I had been in business, I used to write most of the blurbs for the books we published and I had always been adept in so disguising the true character of the book as to make it almost unrecognisable even by the author!

In addition to my books, I had brought with me a copy of *Hugo's Teach Yourself Italian* and I spent some time until the weather got too hot for study, in acquiring the rudiments of the language. There were others on board similarly interested in either acquiring or practising a language and we made an effort to form official language groups for speaking and reading. We had to abandon the attempt, however, for lack of space in which we could foregather.

The other amusement which helped to preserve our sanity was the game of Housey-Housey, also known as Kino and by a score of other names. Each player was given a card containing fifteen assorted numbers; in exchange for a small stake, numbered counters were then drawn out of a hat and the first person to complete their card won the pool. Housey-

Housey is, I believe, the only form of gambling officially countenanced by the army. The other form of gambling that was not countenanced, but almost universally practised, was cards. Solo was by far the most popular game. Chess also had a small and select following. Two tournaments were privately arranged and on most nights some ardent enthusiasts could be seen sitting silently over their boards in some forgotten corner.

Finally, efforts were made, both officially and by the men themselves, to organise concerts. In addition to the amateur and professional talent on board, we had a party of army entertainers whose job was to go round giving entertainments at convalescent homes. Their services were in constant demand. The real obstacle to the holding of concerts was, however, the fact that they were only available to a small audience. It was generally the custom, therefore, to hold them by drafts in turn. A further very important obstacle was the quite surprising lack of talent on board, either amateur or professional. There appeared to be, at most, only one or two of the latter available. And as for the amateurs, they were only tolerated because there were no better alternatives. Let it be hoped that they, like our lecturers, will not be encouraged to indulge in their fancied accomplishments anywhere but under such exceptional conditions as are provided by a ship's concert.

Recreation in the evening was further complicated by the black-out. Of lighted spaces, for the first four weeks, we only had our mess-decks which were hot, crowded and uncomfortable. It was also forbidden to smoke in them. To smoke, one had to go up onto the blacked-out promenade deck, where a popular amusement was to sit outside the doors of the officers' lounge and dining-room, which opened onto the deck, and watch our masters eating, drinking and being relatively merry. Occasionally, some kind-hearted steward would throw the remains of a roll and butter to the patient watchers. Verily the crumbs that fall . . .

Actually, these open doors showed, in my view, a deplorable lack of psychology on the part of the authorities. Nothing rubbed in more effectively the vast distinction between the conditions of the officers and men than this nightly parade. The open doors may have been necessary for the purposes of ventilation. Far better had the inmates suffocated rather than indulged in this ill-considered form of exhibitionism. At the end of four weeks, it was discovered that lights on the promenade deck did not affect the efficacy of the ship's blackout. Instead of being thankful for this blessing, we merely wondered why it had been denied us previously.

I have, I hope, said enough to convince the tax-payer that his money is not spent on idle luxury when troops are transported from one part of our Empire to another, indeed on one occasion, I was moved to write home, 'Life on the German prison-ship, *Altmark*, must be a pleasure cruise compared to the conditions we free citizens endure here'. But this is not to deny that there were some good moments during that trip. There was, for instance, that heart-quickening first morning off the coast of Scotland when the twenty large liners of our convoy were sailing in line ahead and jockeying for their position under the sharp eyes of our escorting warships, who seemed, so numerous and varied were they, to comprise the greater part of the Home Fleet. Our confidence when we saw them became high! It remained so throughout the voyage. The handling of that convoy by the Navy was superb. It was, indeed, a repeated daily thrill to come on deck first thing in the morning and see the huge, sleek outline of the battleship *Nelson* steaming quietly along in our midst, confident in the knowledge that she could easily take on the greater part of the German Fleet single-handed.

Then there was our first port of call, the sun-baked coaling station of Freetown. With it came the tireless pleasure of watching the native boys diving for coins and trying to sell us fruit which, alas, we were forbidden to buy on account of the dangers of infection. There was, apparently, no means of enforcing such an edict against the crew who bought freely and could thus presumably introduce disease on board in spite of our enforced abstinence. But the best moment of all at Freetown was at night, on deck, after the heat of the day. The moon was at her extravagant African best and the whole of the dim mysterious coastline was lit up in fairy enchantment. But greater still by far than the moon were the lights from Freetown, which gleamed out over the water naked and unashamed. They made a poor showing, it is true, but they were the first lights we had seen at night for nearly two years. Sitting on deck and hearing the strains of some distant accordion playing the nostalgic refrain of some popular tune of the moment, it was easy for the time being to imagine oneself in a different place, at a different time, and to forget temporarily the grim purpose of our voyage.

But if Freetown was exciting, Cape Town gave us almost delicious hysteria. We had four days on shore there and they are days I shall never forget. The welcome that was accorded to the troops by the South Africans of, mostly, English descent was, indeed, one of the most moving experiences that I have ever had. While the convoy was in port, every man, woman and child appeared to have only one object: to put himself completely at the disposal of the visiting troops to give them a good time. It was marvellous to see it. No-one, I am sure, from all that convoy who desired hospitality went without it. Then, too, it is easy to picture our feelings after nearly two years of comparative privation in England, and from weeks of confined unpleasantness on the boat, to arrive in a city where every form of food and fruit, which had lately been denied us, was available. Most of us ate well and drank well. But there must have been few who had the strength of will to avoid making themselves sick over the fruit. Grapes, apples, lichees, avocado pears, oranges, pineapples, melons, pears and bananas could all be bought for a trifling sum. Since my schooldays I had not been so greedy, but then I felt like a schoolboy. Cape Town nearly made up for all the discomforts of the voyage. I can give it no higher praise than that.

There is, I think, only one moral that need be drawn from our life on board the *Pasteur*. During war-time, civilians and combatants alike have to endure a great deal of hardship and discomfort. They do it willingly and, in most cases, uncomplainingly. It is perfectly obvious that the urgent need to transport troops to the Middle East, combined with our shortage of shipping space, was going to make overcrowding on the troop-ships unavoidable. No-one, I think, would have complained at this. What I have attempted to show is that much of the discomfort from which we suffered could have been easily avoided with a little imagination on the part of the authorities.

❧

London, SW1

April 23rd, 1941

Darlingest G,

A week ago I was writing to you among the rocks and sunshine of Crinan. My present circumstances are very different, alas! I am doing a night of fire-watching duty sitting in a small room at the top of a very tall house in Chester Square. It is only 11 p.m. and my vigil continues until dawn, which seems an inexpressibly long time. I am not alone, but the other watcher has already done two nights this week and is employed by day so I thought she deserved more sleep than I did and, at present, she is snoozing very peacefully on the bed. Even a sleeping person can be companionable in an empty house with nerves rather touchy in anticipation of sirens. I am then supposed to spring on to the roof and direct fire-fighting activities, but I am convinced, if any bombs fell anywhere within miles, the fire-fighters would have to conduct their own activities!

We left Scotland very reluctantly last week, having missed one of London's worst raids. Luckily the flat was undamaged except for a pane of glass and a few more windows had gone in the house. The crypt of the church where I sheltered last autumn was hit and the poor old vicar was killed. His wife still continues to work her canteen there each night which seems rather plucky! F & M[1] got it not too badly and I hear Quags[2] has followed in the way of the Café de Paris[3]. The damage was fairly general and quite a lot round us. The office has even had to keep open on Sundays to deal with it all, so I am going there every day for a bit.

I try to be very guarded when I write to you as I don't know if our letters to you are censored and, if so, what the censor would regard as an impropriety! Do let me know if gossip is permissible as I am quite sure my veiled allusions would be as mystifying and provoking as the M of I[4] bulletins!

I have just been out on the roof. A piercing wind is blowing and I am very thankful that I don't have to stay there. There seems to be an unusually vast number of stars and very baffling to be whatever the word is that denotes the species who makes stars their hobby. It is now midnight so we are getting on!

---

[1] Fortnum & Mason
[2] Quaglino's Restaurant
[3] Demolished by a bomb
[4] Ministry of Information

Doris[5] is threatening to leave and go into the country as she didn't like the raids last week. Her description of how her face was pulled out like elastic by suction was very funny but she takes it all very seriously. She told me in sepulchral voice as I left tonight that it was exactly a week ago since it happened and how awful if tonight etc. etc. – I am brassily cheerful about it as I find her constant wallowing rather disheartening!

We went to see *Dear Brutus* on Saturday. I found Barrie's sentimentality a rather irritating experience and I kept on wishing he would use his brains more and his emotions (which in his case are usually bogus) a good deal less. It was the usual brilliant company which John Gielgud generally collects.

My letters to you get worse and worse but one's doings seem to be so trivial and one's thoughts more trivial still. Even my work seems to present little that is amusing. I can only think of my interview with a girl this morning who happened to be cockney and toothless, with an agonising stutter! The two poor old Miss Rams[6] have been defeated at last. After a bomb on each side of their house they have decided at last to leave and go to the country. The whole of their lives has centered round their house and garden and it seems horribly sad that they can't spend their final remaining years there in peace. Poor Mrs Storrs (Sir Ronald's sister-in-law) has had to leave her home, too, and has lost nearly everything in it.

I am feeling very sleepy so I shall stop for a bit.

Two nights later

I have not had time to finish this before but I am on duty again, fire-watching, so I can continue. It is not so bad

---

[5] The daily cleaner
[6] War-time neighbours

tonight as I can stay in the flat but I have to keep my clothes on and listen for the siren, if it goes. The other night was divinely peaceful and I quite enjoyed it as the other person was so nice and we enjoyed talking. She is doing medical work and is a few years older than me. We seem to share the same views of books, people, politics, education and 'all' which is always very satisfying.

I have been listening in – for a change! They have been doing extracts from different cinemas including *Seven Sinners* – it wrenched my heart rather to remember we had been there together, not so very long ago. I expect it seems ages to you.

Leslie came across the following verses which I think are rather nice –

> We travelled in the print of older wars;
> Yet all the land was green;
> And love we found, and peace,
> Where fire and war had been.
> They pass and smile, the children of the sword –
> No more the sword they wield;
> And O, how deep the corn
> Along the battlefield!

I must write to Brownie.[7] She wants your address and, also, it was her birthday yesterday.

Well, my very dear one, I must stop and say good-night. I will write again very soon. You are always in my thoughts and I am cultivating a nice, patient trance until this war is over and we can be together again.

Your very loving sister,

D

৵৻৶

---

[7] An old family nanny

London, SW1

May 14th, 1941

My very darling G,

I am beginning this letter to you in rather an exalted state as Leslie and I have been celebrating, in our usual way, the second anniversary of our visit to Paris.[1] We drank a very loving toast to you wishing for your speedy return. After the amazing advent of Hess in Scotland I feel anything and everything is possible!

We did a big 'tidy' in the flat today and Leslie was about to commit your lovely paper-spill to the pile of objects for disposal – I explained it was yours so we decided to keep it in its corner of the fire-place as a symbol, until you can take your place by the fire instead! It will be interesting to unwind the charred remnant and see what date and what news it contains!

I think I told you L's (honorary)[2] spot had been refused? There is a prospect of two other jobs, one in London and the other in the country. We are rather hoping that the latter may be possible as we would prefer it to London, but both jobs would mean more interest and responsibility.

On Saturday we had a very fierce raid. The noise was so appalling it woke us up so we dressed and went out. My reaction to fireworks as an entertainment will be very tepid in future, I think. We spent a lot of time doing a praise-be-to-Allah crouch in the gutter which must have looked very funny and certainly felt quite absurd. We saw a fire blazing in Chester Square and I was very much afraid our fire-fighting services might be required, but it was a gas main and too ambitious for us to tackle. Two houses from Leslie's[3] on the

---

[1] Where they became engaged
[2] Rise in rank
[3] The Gault flat adjoining Eaton Square

33

other side of the Square were also demolished, but luckily they were empty. Ebury Street had several cracks and a warden lost his head (literally, I'm afraid) and there were two in Eaton Square, one killing people sheltering in the trenches. I was very glad when the dawn came at 5 a.m. Next day we went to the Queens for lunch and nobody else appeared until about 3 p.m. – it is very considerate of Hitler to choose a day when we can have a nice 'lie-in' in the morning! Poor London is looking painfully shabby and there seems to have been an awful lot of stuff dropped, but possibly smaller than usual. There was a good deal of damage done round our old flat though the block itself is undamaged.

At last Gaga Mole has seen *A Slight Case of Murder* and simply loved it. We discovered it was on in a small cinema along Edgware Road in a programme with *Angel,* an old Marlene Dietrich film directed by Lubitsch.

It was frightfully exciting to get your letter written from the boat. It must have been rather ghastly and my admiration for the way you have stood it all grows even greater. You seem to be bearing the brunt, more than any of us, of the foulness of this war. We had great competition filling in the gaps made by the censors! Leslie had to censor a letter the other day, written by a man who was C.B.[4] He wrote 32 pages of frightful tripe and Leslie's description of it made me sympathetic with the censors when it comes to my rambling efforts.

Spring really seems to be coming at last. The blossom is out and the trees are turning rather timidly green – somehow the sunshine makes even peace seem less remote. I wonder if you are having dreadful heat. I see in Egypt the temperature has been 117°. It's to be hoped that you are 'sticking to your pants'.[5] Do you remember a day about a year ago when we

---

[4] Confined to barracks
[5] Family quip referring to a constant comment of Pops during any heat wave

went bicycling together in the country? How lovely it was – and is such a precious memory.

I wonder if you will be able to use this new scheme of photographed letters which are supposed to travel quickly. It sounds rather public but would at least fill the void that your absence makes. Your letter made me terribly home-sick for you and disturbed all my philosophical complacency that I had been trying to create!

Good-night. Take great care of your self. Very best love from Gaga Mole and your very loving sister,

D

❧

London SW1

July 6th, 1941

My very darling G,

Your lovely letter, written from the boat, has just arrived. I have read it so often I almost know it by heart and it has made me terribly happy. I miss you desperately all the time and your letter seemed to bring you very close. Now, when I feel particularly lonely for you I shall always have your letter to turn to knowing that I shall always find comfort.

I feel very close to you at night, lying in the darkness praying that we shall both find strength together. I think your idea of sending a message to each other is a wonderful thought and I do believe it would be possible. I wondered how most successfully I could do it, as it is so difficult to imagine your circumstances. I decided that it would be easier if I thought we were back again in Carrington House. I imagine that I am sitting on your bed in the dark and I talk to you about things that have happened or that I'm thinking about, and we decided together that life isn't so bad and 'tomorrow' will come even more gloriously than 'yesterday' seemed. I wonder if time where you are is the same as in England and whether we both go to sleep at the same time? I usually talk to you about 10.30–10.45 p.m. I don't mean this morbidly but if anything should happen to me and there is any power after death, I would come to you and never be far away from you.

In your letter you say the world will inevitably be more disagreeable after the war, but I am not sure that it will. The thing that surprises me most is the incredible adaptability of the human being and it seems to me that whatever the future is it will seem right and natural and the thought of returning to pre-war standards of life would seem almost surprising – like returning to the nursery when you were grown-up. Looking back on childhood is pleasant, and memories are lovely to have, but it seems to me that the war will have changed us into adult people, made us self-reliant and unafraid and, although we will delight in the past, the future and whatever it holds will seem right and satisfying. We can never go back but I doubt, if any of us could, whether we would ever choose to do so! My God – we've been lucky! The things which you were remembering was like listening to an old tune which swings you back to another time and you recapture the utter joy and happiness we have known together. There's not a moment I would have missed, even unhappiness! I passionately want to go on living and feel so curious to know still more of life.

I was delighted by the Oscar Wilde quotations and I intend to read *Dorian Gray*, *National Velvet* and some of the other books you mention. I thought *Theatre* was supposed to be Ivor Novello and his mother, but I don't know.

I hope your food is better now. The bortsch is still waiting for your home-coming! What a dinner we will have!! I can scarcely bear to think of the future when peace has come and you are home again – life seems to have been suspended for the duration of the war and one lives in a state of sub-consciousness, not thinking too much, or feeling too much, with every atom of emotion and vitality pinned on one tiny point of light at the end of the tunnel which life is at present. We live in the same state of tension as though we were sitting waiting for someone, our ears and nerves taut, our hearts scarcely beating, waiting and listening.

I came up to Whitton on Thursday for a long weekend, Hazel came up for the night but only had 24 hours off. It seems odd to be here alone with the parents. No tennis; no joyous rides up the Alwinton Valley; no ice-creams in Alnwick on our way to Sugar Sands; no parties at Cragside or riding through the woods. After the first terror of not knowing what the horse would do it was very pleasant to sit back and let it wander along while the sun shone in patches through the trees and the air was heavy with the scent of pine-trees. The parents are very well and cheerful – I have never seen Mops look so young and pretty for ages. Peter is a little elderly, and when he goes to sleep his tongue hangs out of his black squidgy face like a postage stamp.

It is very much colder here than in London which was hotter than a New York July. Vegetables and fruit are sadly late so from that point of view I have timed my visit badly! Hazel and I bathed in a Cragside lake and found it sur-prisingly warm. Mops sat with a watch in her hand and kept up a running commentary on being late for lunch!

I have discovered the Gault skeleton in the cupboard! An aunt, rather like Aunt Emma[1], who came to tea with me the other day. She goes in for some crazy American religion

---

[1] Pops' sister, a novelist living in Switzerland who was considered a bit eccentric

which takes a keen interest in the physical. Everybody is divided into types and Gaga Mole was very shocked when I told him his aunt said all his troubles came from his genitals! I don't think she will be allowed to come for tea again!

I have been reading a perfectly enthralling book called *Looking for Trouble* by Virginia Cowles, an American journalist. It begins with the Civil War in Spain and goes to the present day. It is an amazing record of events and personalities and very much your 'cup of tea'. Another cable has just come through from you to say you are well but still no mention of having received any of our cables or letters. When I get to London I shall try and make enquiries to find out if the address is inadequate. Incidentally, 'the Captain'[2] was delighted to get his letter from you – it was very sweet of you to write as circumstances and the heat must have made it very difficult.

Leslie is due for leave on July 19th. We tried again for Morar but without success and are trying to go instead to Crinan on the west coast of Scotland. We are both longing to get out of London for a bit of a holiday together, although it has been blessedly peaceful recently. Well, my beloved one – I feel this is a very inadequate letter for all that is in my heart. I can't properly say 'thank you' for being you but you have given me so much richness and now your courage gives me hope and courage, too. God bless you and keep you safe and bring you home soon again.

Always your very devoted,

D

ornament

---

[2] Diana's husband, Leslie

Gunner G.A. Watson 979135,
B Troop, C Battery,
4th R.H.A. – M.E.F.[1]

July 17th, 1941

Darling D,

It is more than a month since I last wrote to you. To tell you the truth I have postponed and further postponed doing so in the hope of hearing from you. Otherwise I could only have written you what I had already penned to the family. But what, in addition, makes letter writing more of a bane than a pleasure is that one's mind is filled with reactions to one's doings which I should like to relate. But as I cannot relate the actions I must also be silent on the reactions. And so any letter to you must be deplorably dull.

I am writing this sitting in the back of a truck which is my travelling home, in the middle of a minor sand-storm which is blowing sand in my hair, my eyes, my nose and my mouth. Life up here is quite incredible. One lives in the truck in which one travels, sleeping beside it and cooking one's own rations. The rations, incidentally, are reasonably good. The principal and most necessary items are four or five daily strong, sweet brews of tea. For breakfast we have bread and tinned sausage or bacon. For lunch bread and cheese. For dinner bully beef, and salmon or herrings or occasionally fresh meat and potatoes or onions or cabbage. Now and then we shoot a gazelle which we cook. Oranges or limes are issued every day and in addition one can buy tinned fruit and beer at the canteen. The water is brackish, but tolerable. It depends where you are how much you get but even up front one can generally get a cupful every three or four days to

---

[1] 4th Royal Horse Artillery, Middle East Force

wash and shave in. In a few days I hope to be going far back to the sea for some time so one will get bathing and clean clothes. The desert itself is an endless expanse of undulating, stony, hard sand with a measles effect of tiny prickly shrubs. There are no trees, oases, or habitations of any sort. The essence of everything is complete mobility so for days on end one only sees the people in neighbouring trucks which are parked at wide distances from each other to be safe from air attack. It is a dreary life. Practically nothing to do, and yet no inclination to do anything to fill the time. In the afternoon one wants to sleep but the flies, which make life a purgatory, prevent this. The flies are hell. I have never seen anything like their persistency. They attack one in hordes. You brush them away and the same flies come straight back like an arrow. Life would be tolerable without them but they prevent all concentration. I play a little chess, read a little and cook and otherwise do nothing. I am lucky in my immediate comrades. On our truck we have a very nice officer, whose assistant I am and whom I help with his work, a charming well-educated Rhodesian of whom there are several in the regiment, all gents. He is wireless operator. And quite a nice driver. On the whole the people in the regiment are quite nice although being in a regiment of regulars they are a mixed lot.

Since I came up here six weeks ago no-one in this troop has received a scratch, and I think we may go back for some long time. And I shan't be sorry. You cannot possibly imagine the demoralising boredom of it all. Still even boredom I suppose is better than fighting.

My love,

devoted G

≈≈

L/Bdr. G.A. Watson 979135
B Troop, C Battery,
4th R.H.A. – M.E.F.

August 4th, 1941

D, darling,

You will see that Watson, at last, has got promotion, by those mysterious figures preceding my name up top. They are the correct way of abbreviating Lance-Bombardier which is the snooty artillery equivalent of the infantry's Lance-Corporal. There is, of course, no honour attached to this acquisition of a stripe. I believe that anyone who is sent to an O.C.T.U.[1] gets one more or less automatically. For this reason it is rather a source of embarrassment to me because naturally – in view of the mob I am with – I am trying to keep as quiet as I can about the O.C.T.U., at any rate till I know definitely when I am going.

Not far from where we are encamped at the moment is the nearest approach to a story-book oasis I have yet come across in the desert. It consists of about a couple of dozen date-palms, a cluster of white, dry-stoned hovels, a little coarse green grass, a few pathetic attempts at cultivated plots and a large number of fig-trees. I had the morning off one day this week and I wandered over there. The dates were hanging in great clusters from the palms but they will not be ripe for another month or so. But, O boy, the figs! I ate about three dozen on the spot and then removed my vest and filled that for transportation home. (The vest has never been the same since.) Those figs were absolutely delicious and, of course, several hundred-weight were going bad on the trees for lack of picking. Such is war! I then wandered round the plots

---

[1] Officer Cadet Training Unit

which I found were full of small juicy water-melons and little tomatoes. I had my fill of those! But one of the curious things about this awful country is that even the food they grow themselves lacks the flavour of similar articles elsewhere. With the exception of the figs which are as good here as anywhere. On the other hand, cucumbers, potatoes, tomatoes, eggs (the size of a pigeon and as plentiful as rice), onions (a glut on the market), chickens etc. etc. are all coarse and tasteless. It seems as if God had put a blight over this country so that nothing fruitful will ever come out of it.

I've been reading with considerable enjoyment this week Hemingway's *A Farewell to Arms*, which I am ashamed to say I've never read before. I was arguing the other day with some-one as to what, if anything, we could put on the credit side of the ledger, out of our army experience. My list consisted of having the opportunity of reading a number of books I would probably have never read otherwise, a visit to Cape Town (which was a thousand times worthwhile) and one to Cairo (which wasn't but which I always wanted to undertake). That is all. All the other items which might be included such as patience, acceptance of one's lot, etc., are not, I believe virtues so much as the result of a deadened feeling which everyone has – reaction to the pre-war nervous strain.

One thing which is rather appalling to contemplate is the war-story bore, after the war. Everyone will, I am sure, insist on telling their own pet stories so that eventually one will probably become bored with retailing one's own. It's an appalling thought! On the other hand I'm keen already to tell you all about mine – and just as keen to hear all yours!

Bless you, D, and keep safe.

G

❧

42

L/Bdr G.A. Watson 979135
B Troop, C Battery
4th R.H.A. – M.E.F.

September 6th, 1941

Darlingest D,

Now and then the army straightens its back, puffs out its whiskers and bumbles 'Inefficiency? Disorganisation? Lack of forethought? Never heard of such a thing. We'll show them how efficient we are.' They then order some perfectly futile form of activity. An example has just occurred here. Yesterday on our notice-board there appeared instructions concerning Christmas postings. Now this would be a splendid piece of foresight if Xmas mail had to be posted home in September. But on reading further one learns that it is quite unnecessary to do anything until November 21st. By which time we shall have forgotten all about the order! Unfortunately, however, I have not shown even that amount of foresight over your birthday. I should, I suppose have written in July. Instead, I will write on the day itself. (I did send you a cable from Cairo, couched, I am afraid, in the same terms as one to Mother. But as the only alternative seems to be either to congratulate you on your promotion or express concern over your confinement,[1] I thought it safe to stick to the beaten path.) What can I say other than to wish you peace, security and safety? What can I hope for on your account other than we should all be together to celebrate it next year. These things I do wish you with all my heart.

I came back from leave yesterday and found a great pile of

---

[1] These army postcards contained only set messages to be ticked
appropriately according to the situation

mail waiting me including three from you – your 2nd, 9th and 10th. Only two are now missing – the 3rd and 8th. Oh, D, if I could only give you some idea of the happiness your letters bring me. I pore over them and re-read them and think about them and I feel as if you were there with me and we were talking together in the flat. You are lying on the sofa in your blue quilted dressing-gown. I am spread-eagled in the arm-chair. While my head may – so it has been suggested by Fifth Columnists – be plastering the cushion with Savoy hair-oil, your feet – as usual bare – are not noticeably sweetening the atmosphere. Your hold-all attache-case is open beside you and as I pass you bills for immediate payment so they are put instantly into it, next day to return to the pile in the desk! I am constantly thinking about you but your letters always conjure up new scenes out of the past which is so very precious to me. How I should have got on out here without you beside me to help me I don't know. Certainly I should have felt lonely. Now I only feel an exasperated urge to get back to all the things that have meaning and abandon all this futility. But I am very lucky. Some of the troops here have not been in England for five years. In the interval their families and relatives and friends have either died or lost touch. Nobody writes to them except impersonal 'pen-pals' round whom they build pathetic romances. They have no roots in England any longer. I have no roots, or interests anywhere else, and the past is the only thing that marks the passing of the week. How blessed I am in my family. How blessed I am in my elder sister.

Quite incidentally, and apart from the personal interest I have in every line, I think your letters are the best letters I have ever read. They are witty, observant, philosophic, graphic and well-written. One gets an admirable picture of life and a very shrewd personal commentary on life from them. I am, of course, for other reasons keeping them all, but apart from those reasons they will be profoundly

44

interesting to re-read after the war. My letters, on the other hand – other faults apart – must suffer from a terrible feeling of restraint. The knowledge, when writing, that you are prohibited from saying certain things – even though one may have no wish to say them – does colour one's whole mode of expression. I find, too, my vocabulary – through ill-use – is getting horribly rusty. Till I met the Phillipses[2] in Cairo I had never *talked* to anyone since leaving my friend Stewart of the boat. Out here one simply chatters.

It was lovely to get to civilisation again and marvellous to find someone from home. Till I met the Phillipses I had had a curious feeling – difficult to describe – that I was the only one from my world who had been transported into this queer sector of the war. It was rather like setting out on a very long journey through a black tunnel with no-one beside you except words of help and encouragement – your letters – from one end. The light at the other end seemed an impossible distance away and sometimes one wondered if one would ever get there. And suddenly, out of the darkness, a hand came out and a friendly voice saying, 'You here, too, Graham. Come along with us.' I'm afraid it's very difficult to explain but *meeting* them was the important thing. I knew in theory that they and Jimmy and Bath-Bun and God-knows-who were all out here, but I never seemed to meet them. Their tunnel might have been a different one and, perhaps, not so dark. It didn't somehow help. Meeting the Phillipses made me know more fully that I hadn't lost temporarily things like the *Observer* crossword, our rivalry to produce better dinners than they did, our excursions into the country. Those things were out here. And with them, too, were all the other things that went with them. Not lost – not even temporarily – just waiting for me to pick them up again when the chance arose. I'm afraid this is hideously involved but I think you'll understand.

---

[2] Old friends from London stationed in Cairo

John was terribly sweet to me. He wanted to see me off but I wouldn't let him. He saw me into my taxi and said rather embarrassedly – 'I hate you going back.' It moved me very much coming from him. People who hide their emotions are much more moving when they show them, I think. I remember so well that night when I left Newcastle in the snow. We were all so determinedly brave and I thought I was going to manage it all right. Then Mother, from the shadow of the doorway, whispered 'Good-bye, my darling.' It made me cry all the way down to Osborne Villas as I stumbled through the snow. It brings a lump to my throat now whenever I think of it.

The M.T.C.[3] is, as far as I can gather, like a girls' school where the predominant, indeed the only, interest is the boys. As most of the 'girls' are thirty or so it's all rather incredible but as they are doing useful work I suppose they are entitled to fight their war in a mad whirl of parties and affairs and young men. For myself I found the atmosphere a little unreal.

Apart from seeing them I did nothing except shop, eat vast quantities of ice-creams, fruit and good food and drink a lot of iced drinks. It was all very pleasant. It is like Shaftesbury Avenue with a lot of notices for abortionists super-imposed.

Well, my darling, I must cease fire. My regards to the Captain and my blessings and love go with this to you.

G

◈

---

[3] Merchanised Transport Corps

Extract from Book Society *by Graham Watson, published by André Deutsch*

With Battleaxe[1] behind us, calm once more descended on the desert. By now I had been appointed assistant to the troop commander, who carried out the function of Observation Post Officer. The observation post was an unarmoured eight hundred-weight truck manned by the OP officer, his assistant (the OP ack), a signaller, who maintained wireless contact with the guns, and the driver. We four lived together, ate together, slept together and worked together and we became a closely integrated little unit. Our task was to get into a position where we could observe enemy activity and, if necessary, direct the fire of the twenty-five pounders positioned some ten miles behind us. For protection we had a Bren carrier containing a dozen members of the Rifle Brigade and one anti-tank gun mounted on its lorry or 'portee'. Of course, the Germans were perfectly aware of the function being carried out by these three vehicles, isolated as they were in miles of empty desert. As a rule they left us in peace, as we did them, for this was a period in the desert war when both sides were building up for the campaign we knew to be coming. Occasionally, however, we received attention from a dive-bombing Stuka. At the sound of an approaching aeroplane we would leap from our vehicles and take refuge behind a foot-high piece of scrub thirty yards away. The belief that the scrub provided any protection was illusory but although we were clearly visible to the pilot as we lay prostrate on the floor of the desert, they never bothered to open up with their machine-guns.

In the afternoons the heat would create a shimmering mirage from which curious shapes would seem to emerge. It was sleeping time and only one of us would keep a desultory

---

[1] An early battle staged to achieve the relief of Torbuk

watch from the roof of the truck. Occasionally a German vehicle which had lost its bearing would emerge from the haze and sheer quickly away. Once a German soldier peered into the back of the truck, unaware that it was British. It didn't occur to anybody to pick him off as he quickly disappeared on his motor-cycle. It was, at that time, a rather peaceable war, more akin, perhaps, to a naval battle with ships idly probing each other's strength. The wide, flat empty expanse of the desert, devoid of all life except for the ubiquitous flies which made life a nightmare, exerted a strong fascination. Before going to sleep, as one lay on the ground beside the truck, one stared up at the purple sky with its shooting stars and listened to the quiet droning of the voices in the laager. But the nights were short. The guns remained in position till last light and had to be back in position by dawn. By the time one had eaten the evening meal and performed the several daily duties there was seldom time for more than four or five hours' sleep.

അൗ

London, SW1

September 17th, 1941

Beloved G,

I am sitting in front of the fire with my toes up on the shabby old pouffe and the curtains drawn. The room is full of flowers which Molly[1] brought up from the country – heavy scented stocks which make me think of Whitton on a summer evening, and also of the flower stall in Curzon Street where I used to buy big bunches of stocks for the big white jar

---

[1] Gaga Mole's sister

in our flat. The bowl at the window is full of brilliant coloured zinnias (do you know what I mean?) which are more in keeping with the autumnal nip in the air.

I am all alone tonight as the Captain is on duty and I feel at last the moment has come when I can write to you in peace and put down some of the pent-up thoughts which I have been longing to tell you.

I have just received your longed for letter written on July 17th.

The part of your letter telling me of your doings gave me a pain in my heart and a futile impotent anger that life could be like this. I can't bear to think of you living in such utterly alien conditions and, in spite of the fact that you never complain, I know how lonely you must feel for all the things you know and love and how utterly bored you must be. I try to get some comfort from the fact that you will get some quite priceless things from it all, which you will be glad of all your days, but I imagine it is the same anguished solace that a mother tries to find as she watches her child playing with fire. My very loving admiration of you grows each moment and my pride in you is almost indecent.

I long to know more about you. It is horrible not to know where you are or who you are with, but I try to remember our promise to have faith and try to bear these horrible months with as much tranquility as possible. I am appalled to know that one of your chief pleasures is a strong brew of tea – it seems to signify more clearly than anything your plight! Not even the spurned Earl Grey variety either!

I have been wondering why some people seem to float through life so easily and so uselessly. I feel rather bitter when I think about them but it seems to me that some people are so shallow that life doesn't trouble them at all, either to castigate them or to reward them. Other people are given a lot to bear so that they can become thinking, sensate people, rich with understanding and a heavenly awareness of life.

Ouspensky used to believe in the parable of the sower where some seeds fell which were quite barren and others which could develop to the full consciousness that man can experience. Otherwise it seems so unfair that feckless people we know should appear to always get away with it. Anne came here for a night last week; was full of a facile charm and friendliness but her egotism and supreme selfishness made me vomit. She does absolutely nothing towards the war or anything else; complains because she has only two maids and two charwomen to look after her, and to contribute to her completely worthless existence, is wondering how most easily she can be made exempt should she be called up for National Service. Even when she came here she used the flat as though it was hers and never even offered to help me turn a mattress! And these sort of people are so supremely sure that they are so beautifully right. I thought of you and raged. While Anne was here she heard from Tom[2] to say he was coming home for good. Only a few minutes before I had been reading your letter and the utter misery that it should be he who was coming home, who had really suffered so little during the war, and not you, was quite unbearable. I made myself believe that it was selfish to want you back and that you were gaining something at no matter what cost and hardship which made the Toms of the world seem sickly by comparison.

Leslie has a horrible habit of going to fetch the letters and the only time I have been known to get out of my bath without goading was when one came from you which he put carefully out of my reach.

I have sent you on behalf of all the family various hampers for Christmas which will probably be a terrible embarrassment to you. There is a food hamper from F & M and another from Harrods with an odd selection of soap,

---

[2] Anne's husband

etc., and also a small make-up parcel of odds and ends of food and toothbrushes and books, etc. Probably most of it will be quite useless but it is impossible to know what you need or want so it seemed best to send a big choice in the hope that some of it would be of use! It's horrible to think of Christmas without you but I like to believe some miracle will happen to end all this horror and bring you back again very soon.

I will go on with the rather boring saga of the last few weeks since last I wrote. On referring to my diary I see it begins with a luncheon at Foyles[3] with Leslie's Aunt Georgia (his batty aunt). It was rather like going out with Aunt Emma – she drew caricatures of the other guests on the tablecloth and kept up a running commentary on Leslie's genitals during all the speeches.

To continue the recital – we had another fire practice and the same stalwart handful extinguished blazing armchairs and incendiary bombs. The number decreases and on nights when Leslie is away I am left entirely alone to man the pump. I think it would be easier to stick one's head firmly under the bedclothes and let Rome burn unimpeded! Kate came to dinner afterwards (incidentally I don't think you have met her but you must).

I have just been having my supper and 'a glass-of'. I am very thankful to Pops for my teetotal background as these nights alone are very tempting to booze oneself into a coma of indifference. Actually on these peaceful nights there is nothing to worry about but in the old days being alone with the mice and beetles was enough to daunt one without the added complication of a possible blitz. The war certainly doesn't allow one to grow molly-coddled (odd word!)

---

[3] Literary luncheons given monthly at the Grosvenor House by the booksellers, Foyles

I went to the Labour Exchange for a job the other day as they seem to be screaming for women. The only thing they could offer me was to take round a mobile bath to the blitzed areas. I was quite entranced with the idea but Gaga Mole seemed to think it was a bit peculiar. I wondered whether I should have to wear a neat, knitted, bathing kit and loofah the various applicants. I am not sure if I would be expected to push it like a Stop-Me[4] or whether I could drive with the bath tucked behind under a tent. I always seem to get rather strange little jobs. Pops and the Captain were so strongly against it, I had to decline, so my name and intimate history remains with the Labour Exchange (and a replica with the National Register), until they can produce another suggestion. I thought of doing Mrs Raymond's library scheme.[5]

We have ordered six bottles of whisky[6] for your return and a good supply of port. Champagne, alas, is not so easy. And the bortsch awaits!

I am suffering acutely from a Voice that sings in the Mews. The signature tune is 'I'll see you again' and each time it is murdered more cruelly and bitterly. It makes me murderous to have my lovely nostalgic memories torn and made grotesque. I remember how you loved it.

Well, my darling G, this seems a terrible screed, so full of words and yet really saying so little of all the things which are in my heart. I long to hear your nice, amused chuckle and ache to see you sprawling in the big chair. I began this letter at 6.45 and it is now nearly 10 o'clock. I love writing to you except, on reading it over, I feel so hideously dissatisfied and tongue-tied. I must go to bed but I shan't leave you as I shall

---

[4] Mobile ice-cream sellers, who called 'Stop me and buy one!'
[5] Mobile libaries in hospitals
[6] From the Wine Society which distributed its remaining stock amongst its members

be talking to you again later on, as I do each night. It's such a joy and comfort my silent communing with you each day and gives me courage to believe and to be patient.

Your very loving,

D

❦

Whitton Grange,
Rothbury

November 22nd , 1941

Very beloved G,

It seems all wrong that I should be here without you so that I shall start a letter to you and talk to you thus, instead.

Pops is having his '40 winks' (an extraordinary understatement of the facts), Mops is lying recumbent on the sofa and has not yet broken wind, but grunts occasionally, Hazel (her shoes off as usual) is doing a crossword crouched over the fire, while Den is reading the nearest approach to the *Daily Mirror* that can be found. You will guess that we have just finished lunch and outside the hills seem like a faded brown photograph with the November mist about them.

I have just been down to the Ram Wood. As I was walking there I felt you were there beside me with your collar turned up and your hands thrust into your pockets. It made me wonder about spiritualism and whether in fact flesh has any real substance. Donne's time theory[1] seemed more satisfying. It was nice to think that it was not in my imagination that you

---

[1] Author of the best-selling book, *Experiment with Time*

were walking beside me but that wherever you had been you had left a permanent presence behind. In a way I feel the same about Peter. I don't feel lonely and empty without him, as I expected, because he does still seem to be here, snuffling among the leaves and scampering down the paths. I miss not being able to snoozle him but that is not so important as the feeling that he is still with us. I vowed to read *Experiment with Time* and really find out what it is all about, and yet I am afraid to, in case it is not so consoling as my interpretation that I have built from only hearing about it, when people have tried to explain it to me. I believe in *Methusalah*, Shaw works out an idea that as a human being develops he can achieve a state of existence first from the physical to the sensuous and from the mental to the spiritual so that in the final state the body simply doesn't matter. If you have read *Methusalah* you will probably realise that I have not, and writhe at my version of it. I say that I must read it but like all these resolutions it will probably remain a hopeful intention.

Hearing about a book and not reading it is sometimes so much better, like a child's conception of paradise – you twist it to fit your own needs and it is probably as far removed from the original as the game of Whispers, where the message is passed from one to another and is quite unrecognisable at the finish. All the same having a body has advantages!

While I have been writing Hazel has turned from her crossword to the composition of poetry which she has just read aloud. Her style is veering towards Auden and Mops feels it is too much Mrs Bowes-Lyons-in-*The-Spectator* to be enjoyable. She confesses that she thought your early sonnet addressed to the gentleman Pig who climbed up a tree called Fig was more comprehensible. 'After all, all you are trying to say is that it was a wet day' was Mops' summing up of the situation!

We are now being entertained by *Musical Moments* on the wireless which will make for a rather distrait letter.

Pops is very chirpy and has returned to the m/s of his thoughts on Life. He wants me to read it and give a true criticism. I rather dread it as I think we both agreed it was not right and he will hate it if I tell him so. Mops is a bit low. Living here out of the war, and being afraid of it, makes her get things out of perspective especially with Den as a perpetual companion, with occasional doses of Aunt Nell[2]. I have persuaded her to come back to London with me on Monday. She can see the shops and theatres and I think the change will do her a power of good and take her thoughts off Peter. His death, in a way, was an outlet and excuse for all her unrest and unhappiness, generally, and a few days of gaiety will put her in a much healthier state of mind. When I proposed it Den said to Mops, 'But surely it wouldn't be safe'. I could have gladly borrowed your wet fish!

The scene that is now taking place would absolutely delight you! Hazel has rashly passed her poem to mummy to read. The conversation is as follows:- Mops: 'A mortal sky? That means dead, you should say leaden.' Hazel: 'The sky was dead.' Mops reading on: 'Her frenzied feet? It doesn't make sense, Hazel.' Hazel: 'She had high heels and was hurrying.' Mops: 'She couldn't hurry, you say her back is curved and bowed.' Hazel: 'Her coat was wet.' D: 'I wonder if Stephen Spender has a mother.' Etc. etc. I can't think why it hasn't been used as a revue sketch.

Last weekend Hazel came to stay. We went to see Leslie Henson in *Up and Doing* with Binnie Hale, Cyril Richards and Pat Burke. Henson was as heavenly as ever, B. Hale looked horribly ravaged, Cyril was good in spite of a snuffly nose and sang a perfect song about the 'Whitehall Warrior' and Pat Burke was competently attractive but seemed to lack passion. I expect you saw it before you left? I told Hazel how we had

[2] Nell, sister of Mops, lived with her mother

met Cyril R. at the Meynells[3], it made me feel very distinguished. On Monday I made my debut at the babies' clinic. I had to sit one on the weighing machine and he immediately sent out a shoot of water like a garden statue and caused consternation among the waiting mothers and their brats who were drenched. It rather shook my nerve. I was hastily transferred to dealing out wool and various food mixtures. My difficulties in working out change were added to by the burden of how many balls made a coupon and not being a furious knitter I think the mothers found my advice precarious. I discovered no information useful to the stud but was rather fascinated by a navel which popped out and in on one of my clients.

On Tuesday I went to the Library at Bart's Hospital. I was taken up by a lift boy who is notoriously batty. He made a few advances which put me into a cold sweat and I heard afterwards that he had invited one of the helpers to go out with him one Sunday afternoon. The work was interesting and I enjoyed it. Mrs Raymond (in charge of Red Cross Library supplies) seems to have aged suddenly. She says business is terrifically good but they can't get supplies. Her husband is the only director left at Chatto & Windus[4] and Tony Tasker[5] is somewhere in the M.E.F.[6] Mrs Raymond says he has become the perfect soldier but I can't help thinking that is one of these maternal delusions, unless the army is very different from its reputation. I was interested to find that none of the patients would touch P.G. Wodehouse since his broadcast from Germany.[7] It is so difficult to connect an author with his books and I had forgotten about it.

---

[3] Laurence and Shirley Meynell, novelists
[4] Book publishers
[5] Mrs Raymond's son
[6] Middle East Force
[7] P.G. Wodehouse, captive in Germany, made a radio broadcast
    considered by many as friendly to the Germans

The next day I started at my canteen at the Royal Free. It was violently hard work and I never felt I wanted to look at food again.

I dread to think what this new move in Syria means, but I am determined not to be frightened by the news and break faith with our pact. Perhaps it will put an end to the war sooner and bring you back home again!

I saw Foggon[8] this afternoon. He really is the perfect gardener with his red pippin cheeks and unemotional timelessness.

Sunday – Whitewell[9]

I am finishing this off in bed so that it can be posted tomorrow. Pops has been having a gala evening. In spite of violent protests from Mops he settled in to reading two of his chapters of his book and became so intoxicated with it all, went romping on through a chapter of the Bible. As usual that made me rather want to cry – so full of memories of childhood associated with it all; the solemnity of family prayers in the drawing-room with everybody seeming so strange and remote and Daddy's grave voice praying for each of us. I never could bear it and used to fly to my room in a collapse of misery. Tonight was so different and yet still the same. Only mummy and me there but Daddy's voice the same, so utterly sincere and meaning it all so much. The chapter he chose was so heartrending because we don't quite know about you and whether tonight you are in the midst of the battle, and the words were so beautiful. I longed for the assurance of the family giggling afterwards.

I think I shall take to reciting in self-defense and then if I see Pops or Hazel approach with that rather exalted and

---

[8] Gardener at Whitton Grange
[9] Pops' town house in Newcastle where he lived during the week

57

determined look I shall start to say my poem rather quickly. I can see family life becoming rather difficult as one by one we take to writing our reminiscences, knowing that our own work will have no other public but each other we will listen with increasing and reciprocal boredom as first one and then other members of the family exhibit their literary talents!

Whitewell seems full of ghosts. I can't think how Pops can bear to live here alone. There is nothing more lonely than a house which once was full. I am sleeping in the blue spare-room. It seems as though we were all huddling together at one end of the house to keep each other company. One should have a house either so big that there always appears to be endless empty space or so small that one can only sigh with blissful relief when the family do depart and the walls sink back to their normal limits.

I must finish this which does not mean that I need say good-night to you, however. I will lie in the dark thinking about you and perhaps you will be able to come and talk to me for a little while.

Perhaps this letter sounds a little morbid but I have got my hurties which is enough to see everything through a rather gloomy distortion.

Bless you, my dearest.

D

L/Bdr. G. Watson 979135
B Troop, C Battery
4th R.H.A. – M.E.F.

December 13th, 1941

Darlingest D,

Today we are in reserve and I am seizing the opportunity – the first since the campaign started – to get a letter off to you. At the moment I am sitting outside, my red braces flaming in the sun. I may say these red braces are the envy of the whole regiment and many are the remarks that have been passed about them. I produced them and wore them for the first time the other day when we were issued with battle-dress. Previously I had worn shorts and a belt. I am enormously attached to them both, by six buttons and very deep grounds of sentiment. I suppose it seems odd to you that I should be wearing battle-dress, but except at midday, it is terrifically cold out here. In the early mornings I wear an overcoat, a scarf, a balaclava, two pairs of gloves and a pullover. It is very tricky getting out of bed at 5 a.m. in the morning while it is still dark. It is made partially easier by the fact that I do not fully undress when going to bed – that is to say I take off my overcoat, my gloves and my boots. Sometimes I take off my scarf, my balaclava, and my socks. Today, we stopped by a pond and I had my first proper wash and change of clothes for a month. Actually the desert – to give it its due – is gloriously clean. I was surprised to find my skin lily white and, my clothes quite presentable. The only thing one is heavy on is socks. I shave about once a week and grow a very classy beard in the interim. With a couple of horns – which if I was married I would probably grow anyhow – I could easily pass for a mountain goat. My hair is superb. I haven't had it cut for two months and I have a long curly bob round the neck. Very 1937 I am sure.

It is very difficult to try and give you any clear-cut picture of this warfare, partly because my thoughts about it aren't yet clear. Certainly it is not as bad as I expected. I dread, for instance, seeing people wounded or killed. The officer I was travelling with was shot and died instantly a foot away from me in the car. I saw one of my greatest friends blown to bits by a shell quite close to me. I felt completely unimpressed by either incident. You must believe this, difficult as it may be to do so, otherwise you will think I am suffering in a way which in fact I'm not. I went right through all the early tank battles of the war, up with the tanks in an armoured car as an O.P.[1] We were shot at by every conceivable weapon and very close they were, too. I was frightened at the time, of course, but not as much as I thought I would be and one very soon got over it. Now one is getting shell sense and beginning to differentiate between the sounds of those near and those that needn't worry you. It is hard to believe that things should leave one so completely unconcerned, but it is true. I'm not trying to write it down to stop you worrying, darling D. I'm being absolutely honest with you. It is, of course, a horrible business but I think the explanation is that one becomes the complete egoist. What doesn't actually affect you personally leaves one more or less unmoved. I suppose it is the law of compensation again. One of the worst features of it all is the stifling boredom. Day after day the same – nothing pleasant in it, nothing pleasant to look forward to except the end of it. Even the minor amenities of life gone – rushed meals, no time to read, write or do anything except push or be pushed. It's that boredom that is hardest to bear. Still, we seem to be doing pretty well and it may be over sooner than I thought it would.

You've been a tremendous help to me, D, during the campaign. I've thought of you – and the family – often when

---

[1] Observation Post – which maintained contact with the guns, by radio

I needed support and help and found great comfort in you. Every night before going to sleep I've tried to tell you I'm still safe and not to worry. I don't know what people do who have no-one to rely on for their lives in times like these.

I'm afraid I have lost a bit of mail since the campaign started. I know for a fact of two bags which were destroyed. Your last letter I got during the middle of the worst of the fighting and what a comfort it was. It was the 16th, written on September 17th. I have now received every one of your first 16 letters. Pretty good for the G.P.O. I think. I do hope that by now you have got some of my letters. I have lost the list but I think this is my fourteenth to you. I have pasted up a very black mark against Gaga Mole for not letting you take the mobile bath unit – a delicious job. His aunt – the congenital aunt – sounds entrancing. Lay in a big stock of whisky. I'm going on the booze in a big way when I get home. I've had nothing to drink for months except two army rum rations – only a thimble-full – and real fire-water but much appreciated as a change from strong tea. We have managed to collect a certain amount of Italian and German food from scuttled vehicles, but not much – the whole army is on that game. But it was very welcome – particularly a big sack of coffee – because our own rations behaved rather peculiarly and we are living on bully and biscuits for a fortnight. It is a diet which is apt to pall. Things are much better now, though. This morning we had sausages and coffee and biscuits and *marmalade* (bags of that because of Palestine oranges). At lunch we had tea, biscuits and cheese (bags of cheese from Australia where most of our food comes from). Tonight we're having tea, bully stew with *onions* (bags of onions from Egypt and Syria) and potatoes (the first for three months). And will have some biscuits and fig jam (tastes like strawberry jam) later in laager. It's odd to think we have most of what you are most short of. Later on in the campaign we ought to get a lot of Italian food as they did in the last.

Please go on writing your lovely long letters and don't worry if you don't hear from me. Writing is difficult and the post uncertain.

I am looking forward anxiously for the Xmas hampers – so are the other members of my car! I shall be with you in spirit.

God bless you and keep you safe.

G

❧

London, SW1

February 1st, 1942

Very beloved G,

Life seems to have been particularly uneventful recently filled by 'the daily round, the common task', as I feel sure Pops would describe it. Everyone seems to be suffering from the inevitable gloom and despondency of winter, and Harold Nicolson's[1] sense of frustration, both individually and nationally, is rife. 'There's a good time coming' – as the song went but one gets damn impatient waiting for it. It seems almost contemptible for we slinking civilians, from our seats of slothful comfort, even to talk of impatience when yours must be white-hot and seething but that you should be suffering infinitely more only adds to my impotent anger with life. As you said in one of your letters this war has no heroic inspiration for stimulus, one bears it with grim disillusionment and horror. Will it be the end of war or will we relapse into a complacent lethargy while greed and ambition grow around us as flagrantly as toadstools, until

---

[1] Politician, broadcaster, journalist and man of letters

dementia seethes up again into this ghastly orgy? There will still be the lice, and still be the decent chaps, who bear the burdens. I don't want to mingle with the feverish gaiety of the pariahs any more than I want to bear anyone else's burdens. I want to make my own cocoon somewhere where the winds of the world can't touch me, a nice escapist's paradise in a corner of the world which has not yet been ruined. I am tired of being a slave to this magnificent civilization, I want to make my own rules for a change. Perhaps the possibility that after the war none of us will be in a position to choose what sort of life we want to lead makes me grasp at my dreams so fearfully.

On Saturday night we were returning rather thankfully to our beddies and Gaga Mole had unaccountably gone to the door to study the night. He heard rushing of water coming from the house and came to warn me that the pipes had burst. Poor Mrs G[2] crept from her ever-so-cosy beddies and donned wellingtons and mackintosh and went to deal with the flood. The water sounded like the Aira Force[3] and was pelting down from Mama G's bathroom into the drawing-room which was rapidly growing to the size of Windermere. The dining-room ceiling was down and the water cascading down into the shelter where the beds were inches deep. We had to crawl on the roof to empty the tanks and turn off the water and salvage what furniture we could from the shelter. Somehow frozen pipes have never seemed to come into my scheme of life; the sort of things which others suffered but to which one was quite immune. It was another unkind disillusionment and made one wonder if equally one might not be smitten with leprosy or possibly goitre. Next day we did our damp and irritated best to eradicate some of the damage and I thought sympathetically of the walrus – 'If

---

[2] D's married name was Gault
[3] A waterfall in the Lake District

seven maids with seven mops swept it for half a year'. Life seemed better after a consuming and vast and leisurely dinner at the Carlton.

I have been twice to the cinema since last I wrote and saw two excellent films, *Citizen Kane* and *The Three Foxes*. Probably you may have read something about the former which was produced by Orson Welles and is supposed to be the life of Hearst. It was brilliantly done and rather exceptional. The other was a very good melodrama with Bette Davis expounding the moral that you can grab everything and still not get what you want.

On Saturday I have to go into University College Hospital for a night. Apparently my insides are slightly out of position which is obstructing this business of having a baby. It is quite a simple thing to put right, so I am told, but I view it with the gravest suspicion. My only consolation is that chloroform is not necessary and that one is given a nice injection of evipan which produces a commendable drowsiness. The Captain very sweetly allowed himself to be subjected to some severe tests and was very haughty when they told him the shape of his sperm was a bit peculiar! My old friend at the library (we are now on terms of closest intimacy and I call her Maud!) tells me that during an anaesthetic one's spirit floats about independently of the body. I will try to direct mine to the M.E. and pay you a brief visit. I wish there was time to warn you in advance so that we could experiment but it would be too involved to explain in a cable. I wonder if dying will be as difficult as marriage and child-bearing have been for me. It never occurred to me that either could produce so many problems!

There was a lovely woman in the bus the other day who, when the conductor asked her for her fare, replied breezily, 'Just charge it to my account.' The conductor, with great presence of mind, said, 'I am sorry, but we have closed all our accounts since the war.' A nice mad-hatter interlude!

When you come home you will be in a position of enormous advantage as there will be so much to tell us which you can't write about. I, on the other hand, laboriously set down for you the most trivial details of our trivial existence and will either have nothing new to tell you or must repeat every stale and indifferent news. Mops rang up to say that a cable had arrived from you saying that you were well, had received parcels (I wonder if you got all three of the Christmas ones?) and were going to see John. This fills me with hope that you may be in a safer place with opportunities to study the Scriptures. It is exasperating to receive such little news of you as I know you must be writing, if it is humanly possible. From what I have heard no letters are coming through from the M.E. just now but I suppose they will be released soon.

Gaga Mole is on duty tonight and it is lovely to talk to you in peace before the fire but there is so little to tell you of any interest. The cold seems to shrivel up one's whole being and although I have a bowl of daffodils on the bookcase to re-assure me, it seems as though Spring would never come! Gaga Mole thinks it would be nice to be a bear eating all summer and snoozing all winter.

I do miss you, my darling, and it makes me so ashamed that I can't share some of your trials and horrors. I am doing absolutely nothing and you are giving everything. I do hope you don't despise me too much. I feel such conflict as to how much my duty lies with Leslie and how much it is my inclination and cowardice which stops me from doing more.

Good-night, my darling – No matter what the distance I am always near you.

My love for always,

D

Next Day

When I woke up this morning I lay in bed wondering if it was worth getting up to see if there were any letters for me – as Leslie was on duty there was no urgency about breakfast – I decided the only letter worth having would be one from you and I thought the chances of that were very few. When I did finally drag myself up I went downstairs to collect the paper and I saw a sight which nearly jerked my heart out of me – a brown envelope. I approached it warily, scarcely daring to hope and prepared for the usual disappointment but it was really your letter! It is no. 13 and dated Nov 16th so goodness knows how much has happened to you since then, but even so, it was heavenly to get it and it may mean the beginning of a flow. The stamp mark was Cairo and dated Dec. 2nd.

I read the passage you quoted from *Ordinary Families* and will re-read the whole book, as I loved it, but have only a hazy memory of it. I can so well imagine that you should feel that only 'now' matters and the future only becomes acceptable because one grows indifferent, but you mustn't feel that and I am sure it isn't true. You must have faith in the future and believe that it is worth waiting for because it is wrong and dangerous to let yourself think that it will only bring disillusionment. Obviously it may hold things different from what we think we want and things which now we can't imagine wanting, but we change ourselves, and our needs and desires change, but not because we become old and sterile but because we have grown and developed into another phase of living. I have always believed that the future was worth waiting for and I have always found it was justified and it makes the present so much more full of meaning. Funnily enough in the book I have been reading there is almost an absolute answer to the theory of Arnot Robertson.[4] In it a child is miserable

---

[4] Author of *Ordinary Families*

because he has become aware that the delights of the present are transitory and even that past pleasure seems meaningless today. His grandmother reminds him that he is not sad because the past is no longer, but because he has changed and no longer wants them, and so it will be again in the future; his sadness for the future is premature as that will bring its own consolations and joys. We hate the thought of change in ourselves because it is unfamiliar, but the change is so gradual that we are scarcely aware that it is happening. G, darling, you must believe in the future and help me to believe in it, too, as without it the war would be too intolerable to bear. While you have faith I am sure the war can't hurt you in any mortal way but if you lose it I think you become vulnerable to defeat. Please, don't give up hope even though life seems worthless because I know that the day will come when all this misery and foulness will fall into the pattern of your life as a preparation for all the loveliness which I feel utterly sure will be yours. I have expressed this so badly and I want so desperately to convince you. It seemed so inevitable that at moments your courage might wane and you have been so brave and borne so much and I can't bear you really to believe that 'now' is all that life will hold for you, even though the world seems doomed and death is so perilously near.

I will answer your letter properly when next I write as I want to send this off now.

I do pray for you, my darling, for now and for always.

D

෴

London, SW1

April 4th, 1942

Beloved G,

I have been floating on air ever since your letter came. It was such heaven to have really recent news of you (it was dated Feb 15th and marked A) and to know that then at least you were in safety and out of the fighting. I am longing to know how long you were staying in Cairo and why you were there but I suppose you either explained in a letter written earlier, which has not yet arrived, or you were not allowed to give particulars. The family received a cable which, as usual, was undated which makes me afraid you are back again in Libya but somehow your letter has given me new hope to face even that horrible eventuality.

I am very relieved that the G.P.O. has dealt so efficiently with my letters to you and I hope it may continue. I wonder if you ever received three parcels posted from London for Xmas which contained an odd assortment of food, chocolates, Mornay's French Fern soap and other knick-knacks for which Mops, Gaga Mole and I contributed and shared? I also sent you off a pullover which will arrive, if ever, when the desert is unbearably hot. From time to time I have sent you cables; some of them official messages and others of my own composition.

Pops has finished his new book and he says he will send me a copy. He says he wants my honest criticism but I doubt if he would actually like to have it. I have asked Eleanor[1] if she would mind looking it through as I thought her judgment would be sound and impartial.

The portrait from Tel Aviv has not yet come and I am

---

[1] One-time publishers' editor

waiting eagerly for it. I have a most attractive snapshot of you on my dressing table which Granny allowed me to have from her collection. It is taken in your room at Cambridge. You are lounging back in that elegant way with your hair discreetly long and a rather sweet little smirk, as if the book you were reading was rather satisfying. The only photographs tolerated in the flat are yours and Peter and the Captain aged eighteen months so you can see what an important place you hold! Granny also gave me one enchanting one of Pops wearing a high collar and looking very resolute, aged about nineteen. She brought them out when I went to see her, when I was in the North, because she resented Nell's monopoly of the conversation – being as deaf as a post she was unable to take part in it and decided this was an excellent counter-attraction. Nell was piqued by this move and finally produced another rival box of photographs to distract me from Granny. I spent a very agitated half hour trying to keep the balance even!

I am glad you had such a good time in Palestine. I loved the architecture of it which seemed to have all the simplicity which the moderns strive for, with none of the affectation. My memories of the country are a little over-shadowed by the hordes of Christian World Cruisers[2] who were with us. How nice to meet the old Survey crowd again. Were any of the ones I met at Brighton there? It would be thrilling if your commission comes through and kept you in Cairo for a bit, but I dare scarcely hope.

The thought that every night you are thinking of me and that I can be near you in thought is a wonderful comfort. It makes the distance between us seem to matter less and makes your absence more bearable. It gives me a very definite sense of your closeness and helps me not to worry so please go on doing it and know that I am doing the same. I read your

---

[2] A tour organised by Pops' church

letters over and over again and it makes me feel as though we had actually been talking to each other and the world seems gay and full of lovely things. I never cease to marvel that you can write such wonderful letters in such devastating conditions and am so very thankful for them. I sent you off a photographic letter this morning as they seem to get there quicker but it is impossible to send any news in them. There is so much to tell you, as it is three weeks since I last had a chance of writing. The most satisfactory times are when I can settle down for a few uninterrupted hours so I usually choose a time when Gaga M. is on duty, but the last two occasions Magin has come up to spend the night with me. She seems very happy and is quite unchanged. Her choice of diet is still a bit individual. Her menu for lunch when she was alone was sandwiches and coffee followed by ice-cream and then a Welsh rarebit and after that mushrooms on toast and a final ice-cream! We went to see Shaw's *Doctor's Dilemma* together, which was superb.

I had a lovely time in the North and it is very satisfying to find the parents so perfectly unchanged. Pops took me out for a long walk in a high wind at Rothbury. I was anxious to know his views on some topic but he had obviously got it scheduled for theorising along his own lines on a quite different subject. He very adroitly changed my conversation into his and had a free run for about twenty minutes. By that time I was feeling rather restive and finally he inserted into the monologue a series of questions and answers which he introduced by saying, 'Now you would ask me ..., and I would say no, you are wrong ...' etc. This was a bit much, so I said firmly, 'Look here, Pops, as I am here why don't you ask me instead of assuming perfectly erroneous suggestions.' He swiftly brushed that aside and continued the harangue. I wish I hadn't inherited the Watson love for talking and then I would be a more docile listener!

The Labour Exchange suddenly roused itself out of its

torpor and asked me to do factory work at a place which was making soldiers' equipment and was in urgent need of women. I had a look at the factory and was greatly attracted by the suggestion. There was no machinery and one could sit down which seemed an advantage; the hours were 2–6 p.m. which seemed reasonable and no objection would be made if I wanted to go away for Leslie's leave. I have been going there all week and was actually presented with my first pay packet on Friday. I have decided to buy a hat with it which Gaga Mole's lunar mathematical sense has predicted will ensure a heavy loss. The hat is 5 gns and the wages were 18/5d (I have always thought there was big money in factories but apparently I have struck the wrong one). My bus fares are 8d a day but if I bicycle I can save that. The famous pride-of-the-Calderwood-hands are suffering a severe set-back and cause me acute agony but I am told that time brings its own horny and calloused reward and is an excellent preparation for playing the harp. I have never felt an urge for harp-playing but perhaps the tendency may develop. I sit in a large room with about 100 other people and a loud radio at a table where about 12 of us work. Our present job is solar topees and I began with linings which is relatively simple but have not to cope with the band outside. It is purely decorative and quite useless and involves colossal labour. There are 21 pins which must be placed in such a way that they don't pierce through to the head and can't be observed by the acute regard of the foreman. You talked of lunacy and surely it was prophetic when you consider my contribution to the war effort is sticking pins into solar topees. Always through life I have discovered that whatever I do I always seemed to do very much less successfully than anyone else similarly occupied. I seem to have no natural aptitudes whether it is playing cricket, doing sums or sticking in pins. We are paid 1/- an hour but soon we are going to be put on piece-work and I have worked out at my present rate of out-put I shall be 1/5d a week to the good which is rather a shaming claim, surely? The girls I work with are extremely pleasant and friendly and obviously do not regard me as a serious threat of black-leg labour. They are enormously interesting and make me horribly ashamed of the complacency of one's own class. Money to them is the very essence of life and even ten minutes to chat to the foreman is totted up in terms of over-time pay. Their interests are entirely personal and sensible. There are two other women of one's own kind. One is a charming person of about my own age and doing it for similar motives. The other is older and as soon as she has finished pin-pushing rushes off to her club where she plays poker until early hours in the morning. She is most unpopular as she has not yet learned that the poorer classes have no sense of possession and are equally quick to take, as to share, so can't understand her rather stupid complaints that someone is sitting on her stool or has taken her tools, which are actually common property. We pay ½d for our tea for which we provide our own mugs and a hunk of cake. The worst problem is the ghastly wireless which continues unceasingly, and at an appalling volume, and the rather peculiar smell which one wonders how much is human and how much ammonia and other contributing processes to topee making. It is very satisfying to feel at last I am doing something which is directly connected with the war and makes me feel less of a swine when I think of all you have to bear. Some idle moment you might spend in unpicking your hat!

I wonder if you have read about Garvin's[3] abrupt dismissal from the *Observer*. Apparently a disagreement with Astor over policy and now he is writing articles for the *Sunday Express*! I wonder what Viola Garvin is doing about it.

Two 'leading publishers' are being prosecuted for indecent publications. The names are not known yet.

I have been writing ever since 8.20 and it is now getting on

---

[3] The long-standing editor

for mid-night so I think I will stop this and finish it off tomorrow when my brain and hand are more agile. I shall go on talking to you in a sort of soliloquy until I go to sleep. I wish I didn't miss you quite so dreadfully. May God bless you always and keep you very safe.

Next Morning

Today is Easter Sunday and tomorrow is a holiday for both of us which is rather heaven. We are celebrating it by going to see Constance Cummings in *Skylark*. It's funny how life has its own ideas about keeping one on the straight and narrow. All my instincts are to be idle, luxurious and pampered. When I sweated round at the A.P.A.[4], and all my various jobs, I always looked forward to being married and a time when I could relax into being the sort of woman who had breakfast in bed in alluring negligee and had her face done at Elizabeth Arden. Instead of which I do my housework, work in a factory and come home and cook our dinner. I must say I still long for my dreams of idleness, even though they will probably never come true, and always having grubby hands and broken nails and wearing old serviceable clothes hasn't quenched my longing for the lovely feminine things of life.

Incidentally, poor Mops will be having a trying time explaining the exploits of her family. You, without a commission, and her daughter a factory hand! I can hear her telling her pals that I don't really need the money and that anyhow it is only part-time!

After a rather depressing winter everyone is beginning to buck up again and taking a more cheerful view of our prospects. The almond blossom is out and I have some branches of it in the flat. It looks too fragile and beautiful to be real and yet the smell of it is like honey and makes one

---

[4] All People's Association where Diana was employed pre-war

think of the country lying peacefully under hot blue skies and sunshine and listening to bees bumbling among the flowers.

I seem to have wandered on longer than usual and I hate having to stop but I seem to have told you all the news and I must write to the parents. I will write again very soon and, meanwhile, I shall always be thinking of you.

Your doting sister,

D

❧❧

L/Bdr. G. Watson 979135
B Troop, C Battery
4th R.H.A. – M.E.F.

June 20th, 1942

Darlingest D,

In spite of the fact that my last letter to you was written over a month ago – May 13th to be precise – this will, I am afraid, be a scant and poverty-stricken effort. At the moment one's thoughts are not in such a state as to make letter-writing other than a hopelessly difficult up-hill task. The thing which has made this campaign so considerably worse than the last is the weather and the hours. Last winter it was dark between 6 and 6 and thus fighting was restricted to a twelve hour day. One got more sleep than was necessary. Whereas now we are on the job at 5 a.m. and continue without a break till 9.45 p.m. Rations and water etc. have then to be drawn and if one is in bed before 11.30 it is a matter for congratulations. Five and a half hours sleep under the circumstances is not enough. Sleep during the day, on the other hand is equally difficult. Although things quieten down as a rule between 1 – 5 in the afternoon, the flies and heat make sleep difficult to achieve. In fact, the general opinion seems to be definitely opposed to campaigning in such weather! I agree. As to my own experiences, I have had some extraordinary adventures about which I will tell you in due course. Meanwhile, I am – thank God – still sound in life and limb.

The cable which arrived announcing young Gault[1] was one of the really thrilling, joyous events of recent months. I cannot tell you how delighted I am for both of you. I had no opportunity of cabling you my congratulations – and in any event a cable is quite inadequate to express what I feel about it. My nephew – or niece – will, however, be but one more incentive to return. Oh, D. I'm so terribly glad and I can imagine how happy you will be.

I also got a letter of yours, 33rd – of April 18th. I loved hearing about your factory experiences. You must find it quite amusing.

Probably long after this campaign is over when I am back enjoying myself in civilisation, you will get a dearth of letters from me and wonder what's happened. But please realise that at the moment I cannot do much about it.

This is a pitiful little note but it will tell you how much I love you all. I feel this war will soon be over and then back to sanity and life. O may it be soon. Till then, look after yourself and young Gault. My blessings and prayers go out to you.

Your devoted brother,

G

❧❧

---

[1] Diana's first son

London, SW1

July 5th, 1942

Most beloved G,

I feel rather ashamed I have been so long in writing since my last letter but these last two weeks have been very sterile in news, action or thought. Actually, the only inspiration was an unexpected and particularly satisfying letter from you (April 11th) which had been enclosed in one to Mops. It arrived on Monday when the news of the fighting in the desert was about as bad as it could be and in it you tried to explain that the reality of fighting was very different to the imagination and telling me not to worry. It could not have come at a better moment and I felt almost as if you were talking to me and letting me know that however bad things were I must believe you would be all right. It was a heavenly relief and I felt as though some kind destiny had arranged for it to come at that particular time and I believed it was an omen that you would be looked after and kept safe.

I am glad you are in no way changed. Actually, I knew from your letters that you had not altered, or at least in any way that would make you seem a stranger. Your list of discoveries are interesting. I agree with all that you say about the privileged classes although there are naturally exceptions. But, as a generalisation, it is just as well that we will be quietly disposed of before we can continue to grow increasingly objectionable and develop an even greater egoism of complacency. I have not discovered that physical comfort is an illusion but I am sure it must be a most profitable experience to have lost!

And of your remarks concerning real happiness and help to bear the worst, I am absolutely in accord.

You would have laughed if you had seen me this morning. I was going round the flat on my hands and knees busily

76

doing my chores and planning to write you a letter of farewell in case death should 'take me' before you came home. I was so moved by it all that the tears were streaming down my face at the sorrow of the situation. The only thing is that I should never now be able to compose such an epistle without laughing heartily!

This business of pregnancy is extraordinarily interesting. I spend a considerable amount of time cursing the limitations it causes and loathing its very unaesthetic function but then there are moments to compensate when one feels such a sense of surprised and utter satisfaction. When the Mole emerges I shall feel horribly lonely without him. At present we are such complete buddies, in fact quite inseparable, but later he will be an individual with separate desires and an unknown personality. He will be something which inevitably one will love; he will be vulnerable to life and all one can do will be to stand by helplessly watching. Now, to me he is a person, but with no fears for his safety as nothing can touch or hurt him. I regard the future with the greatest apprehension!

We have practically decided to leave the flat next September or October. During this last month or two it has been terribly hot and I have been very much more at home than last year. It has seemed terribly cramped and stuffy and I have gazed up at the chink of sky which one can see above the roof tops in increasing frenzy and shut the windows in a frantic effort to shut out the assault of three wirelesses. One beastly child who sings, 'You are my heart's desire' with a register of five rather undecided notes, as well as the Army on the other side. We are planning to go to Stephen Runciman's house which we can take on a monthly basis. It is in St John's Wood which is rather distant but is suitably small, attractively furnished and possesses a garden. Another advantage is that it should not be too expensive as he only wants expenses paid. At present he is in Persia and unlikely to return for several years.

Leslie is due for leave next week and is joining me in the North and we are going to Embleton for a few days. God knows why as there is no bathing, golf or fishing and one can imagine the pub! It was difficult to find anywhere as the hotels to which I wrote showed good Northumbrian indifference by not replying and it seemed hard on Leslie to surround him with in-laws for the whole of his holiday. We will spend a day or two at Whitton at the end of our leave. Pops was very funny about it. He offered with breezy lavishness to fix up the whole business of reserving a room and told me to ring him up without fail and he would tell me the result. When I rang up it was obvious that the whole matter had been completely forgotten but he hastily lied heavily and said he had thought it would be better to leave it over for a day or two. Finally Mops got it all fixed with typical efficiency. It must be maddening for a king of industry to realise that his wife is infinitely more business-like and capable than himself!

We have a lovely plan for August to go and stay at a place called Stoke Court Club near Stoke Pogis. Leslie will be able to travel in to work each day and it has a lovely garden so the Mole and I can be divinely idle and lead a very properly pre-natal existence together. The place seemed very full of old ladies of every sex, has a swimming pool and a putting green, and is a lovely old country house. It will be utter heaven to be waited on and have nothing to think of for a bit though it makes me feel horribly selfish. I thought I would try and persuade Mops to come and join me for a bit.

Next Day

I must try and finish this while I am waiting for Nancy[1] so that I can post it before I go north. She is coming to tea and is almost an hour late already.

---

[1] Local friend

I have been sticking down and addressing endless envelopes for Mrs Storrs[2]. She is one of the most soulless women I know and a very typical product of Roedean. The theory there was to keep everyone so busy that they had no time for 'nasty thoughts' so we were kept going in a whirl of useless activity with no chance of any thought at all. Mrs Storrs has carried on the Roedean tradition and is on every committee for 'good works' in London, regardless of whether they are any good or not, and is far too busy for even the smallest flicker of Christian kindness or warmth.

Did I tell you I had read *The Last Enemy* by an R.A.F. lad who is now invalided out. It was very moving and worth reading if you have the chance. I have also been reading *The Death of a Moth* by Virginia Woolf and have come to the conclusion she is one of the very finest writers of today.

I haven't said anything about the battle raging near Egypt although, needless to say, it is never out of my thoughts but what can one say that is anything like adequate? At the heart of everything that I do or see is the thought that you are in it. I feel that you are getting through, and that I should know if anything were to happen to you, but the longing to have you back safely again is agony. It is hideously difficult to be patient but as surely as all the other if lesser horrors, have passed and the end of waiting has come, so must this pass too. Still I miss you hideously.

This is a bad letter but I will try and write from Rothbury and send you some of the family gossip.

My prayers and thoughts are always with you.

Your loving sister,

D

꙳꙳

---

[2] Wife of Sir Roland, a distinguished diplomat

July 14th, 1942

D, my darlingest,

Having been more or less mail-less for some months or so you can imagine my joy at receiving a big stack of letters and books yesterday including – from you – three letters (33, 34 and 35) and the *Screw Tape Letters*. Thus your incredible record is still maintained. I have received 35 out of 35! I fully expected that some of my mail would have gone astray in the present campaign. I haven't had time as yet to do more than glance at *Screw Tape* but it is obviously going to be enormous fun. Thank you very much for it. The great news, of course, was the first details – other than your cable – of the arrival of young Mole. I am already devoted to him. Any child that has been sent down a permanent menu of cocoa and sardines is right in cribbing but I should take a strong line over the bus question. This is plainly temperament, and should be discouraged. Hazel, in one of her letters, said that your conversations were far funnier than Gubbins[1] with his stomach. She is perfectly right. I have never laughed so much as over your letters. Any child who grows up in that atmosphere will have the world at his feet. Me, at any rate. Incidentally, I can't easily say how happy the advent of young Mole has made me. *Do* take care of yourself.

I am afraid I can no longer continue the Town & Country argument. Your answers are far too convincing. Naturally I think that most of my arguments were put forward to convince myself if possible because I confess that at the

---

[1] *Sunday Express* columnist

80

moment I crave for a country existence and my pub sounds heaven. But all the time my conscience keeps saying you're an idealist, look at the facts! Actually, the greatest snag is that I am unmarried and I think solitary grandeur would be a bit lonely and I would have few chances of meeting a worthy damsel. But your argument which is unanswerable is: if it doesn't work, do something else. You're not tied to any rural destiny if you don't want it, which, of course, is true. What is Gaga M. going to do after the war? I should love to join him in something if it could be arranged – and, incidentally, if the idea also appealed to him! Perhaps he could become my bar-tender – or a ghillie? I leave it to him which he chooses.

We are nearing the end of our fourth continuous month in the desert. The last two have been the most testing I have ever experienced – physically, mentally, spiritually. Some-times I have wondered whether I could go on any longer. The hardest part, however, has been that I have gradually begun to wonder whether it was all worth anything. I have lost what faith I ever had in our leaders. They have misgoverned us, lied to us, betrayed us. I have met numerous colonials (Indians, Rhodesians, New Zealanders), and they all say we have made a mess of the Empire and that the remaining links are commercial, sentimental and naval. I have lost any faith I ever had in the General Staff. As Churchill said, we started with more men and more equipment than the Germans but we have been completely outclassed – I'll give you details one day. I've lost all faith in our officers who share one redeeming quality, courage. Otherwise, they mostly regard the war as a sporting contest in which the ranks play the part of 'beaters'. I have lost all faith in the upper classes who are not, from what I can judge, pulling their weight in England. The Germans are not, from what I have seen, sadistic maniacs. Do I believe my own eyes or the accounts of refugees which may be tinged – as is everything – with propaganda. (I believe, and hate, what I have heard about concentration camps, but is their price worse than the price we are paying to get rid of them?) I believe utterly in the ordinary decent Englishman and it is for him I am willing to go on fighting. But as they all say: what have we to lose from the war, or gain by winning it? I cannot answer them except in humanitarian terms which don't impress. If you don't believe me, I could convince you they have mostly nothing to lose, but it is outside the scope of a letter. In fact, my darling D, (and if the censor sees this I hope he won't cut it out) our morale is low. Chiefly it's due to too much of the desert and when we get back to Cairo which, there are rumours, will not be long delayed, we will all feel much better. But Pops is mistaken if he thinks I am going to take a 'hand' in reconstructing the new world. The reconstruction and the result will be as phoney as the last (men don't change). So Wogger is going to take himself to the sign of the Rod and Luncheon Basket – the world forgetting, by the world forgot – and make rude noises at young Mole and play with his mother and father. And don't write and lecture me about the dangers of disillusionment, it's a phase that will pass – possibly! – as soon as I get a plate of *lobster cardinal* in the old tum.

I am worried that I have not yet managed to write to Mole senior. Please do explain – as I am sure he knows – that I expect him to be the part recipient of part of my letters to you.

I can't tell you how yearningly I long to see you again, maybe it won't be very long now. Meantime, your letters are a source of joy, courage and inspiration to me.

Yours, as of yore, now and ever will be

G

✍✍

Extract from Book Society:

Our stay in the delta was brief. The troops who had relieved us were new to the ways of the desert and were once more in retreat. They were driven all the way back to the fortified line at Gazala, not far from Tobruk. Here both sides paused for breath. Our new role was to man a fortified 'box' deep in the south below the Gazala line, near Bir Hacheim, which was soon to get notoriety in the world's press through its suicidal defence by the Free French. In May the Germans suddenly struck round this southern flank and what came to be known sardonically amongst the troops as the Gazala Gallop had begun. If the powers that be guessed at the enemy's intentions, it is fair to say that we didn't. I still remember the surprise of suddenly finding ourselves next to a German staff car with a soldier poking a gun at us and saying, 'You are my prisoners.' 'Oh, fuck off,' said the sergeant in charge of our truck. And fuck off they did, and so did we. I never knew why the Germans didn't fire at our disappearing backs.

The ensuing days of retreat to El Alamein are well chronicled. They were depressing for those who took part. So much ground had been won. And now so much ground had been lost. Morale was at a low ebb. In due course we all settled down on the strong defensive line which stretched from the coast at El Alamein to Qattara Depression, a bare forty miles from Alexandria. Here both forces paused for breath, the Germans and Italians with a supply line stretched to the limit, the British to reorganise and re-equip. C Battery once more occupied a position on the south of the line and from here got involved in the sharp and important battle of Alam el Halfa which took place in August. It was Rommel's last attempt to smash the British and my last engagement with the 4th R.H.A. Immediately thereafter I was informed that my papers, approving the application for a commission, made two years previously, had at last caught up with me. I was ordered to return forthwith to Alexandria.

At the time, and subsequently in retrospect, I was not convinced that changing the status of a lance-bombardier (acting and unpaid) for that of a second-lieutenant was a step in the right direction. I was proud to be a lowly member of such a distinguished and battle-proven regiment. My regret was compounded when I discovered that my accursed short sight meant that my medical category was down-graded. There was a certain irony in the thought that I had passed much of my war at an observation post where an essential requirement was reliable vision. Now I was down-graded medically so that only a commission in a less combative unit was open to me. So I was posted to an O.C.T.U.[1] in Palestine to train in the ways of the Royal Army Service Corps.

Rothbury,
Northumberland

July 16th, 1942

My darlingest G,

Your letter F (dated May 13th) came as a heavenly surprise and was a lovely letter. I am so glad you like my letters and it is such a relief to know you think I have a sense of humour as, after much contact with Den and the parents, I begin to grow morbidly convinced that I am utterly bereft of anything but a rather unpleasant streak of malice – 'rather a smell about it' kind. I love writing to you and I unleash all my pent up thoughts to you because I know you will understand and see

---

[1] Officer Cadet Training Unit

things like I do and to get your letters is such an utter joy because it's like the other half of a conversation with you. I think writing is easy when you can do it as you would talk, without explanations or unnecessary emphasis but there are so few people to whom you can write like that. Leslie forwarded your letter on to me here so I had to read out a few suitable bits and gave a rather abridged version of the rest.

It is paradoxical that at home where one is assured of unwavering love one should feel so completely small and stupid – no wonder girls turn to young men for assurance! I know the parents love, with unswerving loyalty, but not only do they not know me as an individual they would go to any lengths to deny me individuality. Primarily I am loved because I am their daughter, and as a human being, I can beat my personality (such as it is) against this resolution to ignore it and make not the slightest impression. It makes me feel frustrated and baffled because as I grow and alter I find the mould which has been allotted to me is the wrong shape, but every time I return to the family embrace I am fitted firmly back into the same design of the rather undistinguished married daughter. I sometimes long to be loved less, but more intelligently!

I have been thinking a lot about your future after the war. I haven't had a chance to broach the subject to Gaga M. but I do know this that he has complete faith in your ability to make a success, as well as utter confidence in you as a person. I am so thankful and happy that you and he are so genuinely fond of one another and do understand and appreciate each other, too. I couldn't have borne it if it had been otherwise as it would be like having my heart torn in two. It is very difficult for me to think about it dispassionately as my own feelings keep on getting in the way. I can picture you being married to an attractive wife, living in a pleasant house and entertaining intelligently. At times you would long for your freedom and you would be exasperated by the people you

85

met and the parties you attended, but you would have money to make what freedom you have comfortable and pleasant and you would find security and numerous compensations in your life.

I see another picture, probably rather rose-coloured and romantic because it appeals to me so much. I see you in your pub living not far from us in Scotland: it is small and white-washed and doesn't hold many visitors so you don't find your duties as landlord very binding and you don't make much money! Out of season you shut it up and go wandering in towns and abroad, mouching about getting ideas and impressions which you translate into writing which is an additional source of income for you. You have a wife, not madly smart, but a nice person who likes your Scottish pub even in the mists and long winter evenings. Whenever you are bored, and want a meal, you come and have one on us and we are always coming to you to pinch some bottles of beer and have a gossip. We would go out sailing together up among the islands, we would fish and try unsuccessfully to sell our garden produce and make the yokels like us a little. Occasionally we would meet in London surprised to see each other looking so soigné but as the years passed we might grow rather lazy about visits and be rather glad to get away from the clamour and back to the sea and the gulls and the loch among the moors. I don't suppose you would be very rich but I can imagine your face would have that happy, amused look which townsfolk don't have. From a worldly point of view you would be wasting yourself and yet I think you would be fulfilled and satisfied. I know I am prejudiced so much that my opinion is almost valueless, but on the other hand one has to be honest about the doubts that are in your mind as to the practicality of such a life.

We have been brought up in a period when the beginning and end of life was to get a job and 'to get on'. We have been brought up in a class where leisure was a luxury and regarded with distrust and suspicion; our father is a man who has driven himself all his life haunted by necessity and his rigid Puritan instincts. We have never paused to realise that people can exist without this discipline of a daily and yearly routine and that such people who have ignored the routine are happy even though they are not providing the nation with vast incomes to tax. To my mind if you can be happy leading that sort of care-free existence there is no comparison to the other. I think you could be happy if you trusted your instincts, but I may be wrong. It seems to me to have the chance of choosing freedom or machine-made servitude is so lucky that it's crazy to choose bondage simply because that is what you know, whereas the other is a hazard. Another thing I realise is that marriage makes the choice easier as it provides you with companionship and less dependence on others. It is obviously easier to find a wife in London than in the wilds of Scotland, but once you are fixed with a wife you will never be able to escape the grind-stone (unless you have done it before marriage) unless she is a very exceptional woman! Gaga M. is moving all his shipping interests and office to Fort William[1] and his secretary is thrilled at the thought of living there! Gaga can potter in a few days a week and do a good deal by telephone – not the way to make fortunes, but why work 5½ days a week with one fortnight in the year for a holiday if you become a sort of robot? A cabbage seems a happier fate!

I'm afraid I am back on my old theme again. It pops up everywhere and I do apologise for being such a bore but the picture of you in your Harris tweeds and a pipe was too much for me!

The Mass in which your name is mentioned is held in the Cathedral in Newcastle. I don't know who the group of people are as I prefer to think of them as probably they are

_____
[1] He did not!

87

not – detached and saint-like. One of them is a woman whose son was at sea on a boat which was reported sunk and she found so much strength in the knowledge of their prayers and sympathy that she wanted to share it. I think they sound genuine but so often those sort of people are embarrassing in their fervour, so I was a little afraid of them. I send messages to encourage them and to express my very sincere gratitude for their trouble and interest.

I feel quite sure that being in the ranks and really understanding the men will be an experience that will be more worthwhile than any other the war could give you. I bet you are proud that you made them like you and it makes me proud, too, as I know what you would be up against to do it!

Your letters have been coming through awfully well. I have all of the lettered series as far as F and the only ones that are missing were some of the earlier numbered ones. I haven't got my list or I could tell you which exactly.

In spite of my earlier complaints about the family, it is lovely to be here again. It seems an odd sort of summer with the tennis court unmarked, and to be here alone. No rushing off to Alnmouth to meet Neville or Nancy. No expeditions to Sugar Sands with dollops of ice-cream en route. No frigid plunges into the icy brown pools in the Alwinton valley. I miss Peter terribly and to have a cold vindictive cat walking in his place seems an absolute blasphemy.

In the mornings we go for rather genteel, little walks. We take a large basket and every piece of wood we see Mops decides must be brought back for fire-lighting. I would resent these sadistic excursions less bitterly if we were not aware that while we labour for a handful of sticks the Huishes[2] are taking our coal to burn. Their fire burns as persistently as the flame at the Arc de Triomphe. It is chilly, so we huddle in the sitting room wrapped in rugs in the

---

[2] The family who were caretakers and gardeners

afternoon and after tea another gentle potter round the gardens. It is deliciously idle and elderly habits seem to suit the Mole. Yesterday some pals of Mops came to tea and we played bridge. I sat ashamed to think that during such a war four able-bodied women could sit in the afternoon and occupy themselves in a way so unworthy.

The general attitude to war-work is utterly appalling and makes me feel like an old colonel discussing the younger generation. Nobody seems to do it, glad that they can contribute something, but only because it is forced upon them. It frightens me that as a nation we seem only engrossed in who can grab the easiest job and perform it as perfunctorily as possible with no other consideration at all. How can the world find peace if that's the spirit of progress.

Pops was very funny about Eleanor's criticism. As it was fairly severe I only quoted the general view and told him he could see the whole report if he wanted to. I think he was disappointed it was unfavourable and he never asked to know the whole report. I am afraid both Eleanor and my efforts have been rather fruitless! Donaldson,[3] of course, was very flattering about it. Uncle Charlton gave a very restrained criticism and I don't know who else has read it but Pops seems to be sending it round to all his pals – all of whom are obviously most unsuited to give an impartial opinion.

Rothbury seems untouched by the war. There is corn growing on the golf-course which looks surprising but one assumes it is malevolence on the part of Proctor[4] rather than any gesture of patriotism.

I am going to Newcastle tonight to meet the Captain and tomorrow we are going off to Embleton. Our return to Rothbury will depend on the degree of discomfort there.

---

[3] Pops' minister
[4] The local farmer

I won't post this immediately as there may be some gossip to add to it later.

With all my love and blessings.
Your most devoted sister,

D

❧

Cadet Watson G. 979135
R.A.S.C.[1] Training School, M.E.F.

September 13th, 1942

Darlingest,

It was a tremendous thrill receiving yesterday your letter of July 16th (No 39) the first I have had for six weeks. Both 37 and 38 have not turned up. I can't bear to think of them wandering round the desert somewhere. Perhaps they may turn up later. I was longing to get a letter from you.

You are, of course, a perfect devil with your insidious propaganda. I look outside my window. Twenty yards away across a wilderness of soft sand I see a wooden army hut. Then I read in your letter of a small whitewashed building nestling at the foot of a loch; of fishing expeditions; of sailing among the islands. How can you expect a man to keep his sense of proportion! Another letter like that and I'll be writing to John Dawson[2] asking him to buy the Morar pub at any price. As to this and Leslie's scheme – which is as attractive and, I suspect, as impracticable as your pub – I have written at length to Leslie in a letter enclosed. No doubt he

---

[1] Royal Army Service Corps
[2] My accountant

will show it to you and I will not repeat myself. But now to some extent we've all got the setting of the stage, we know the players; we've got the backer; surely our combined inventiveness will succeed in writing a script that will fulfil the requirements of the players, the theatre, and the scenery.

Can you honestly, D, see much hope for the world? People change the needle in the gramophone but they're still going on playing the same old record – even if it is a bit cracked, and it's still the same old gramophone. People, and the best of them, too, the ones who really have made sacrifices, are going to arrive home, dust their hands, kick their battle-dresses over the quay-side and say, 'Well, that dirty job is finished. Let's go to the Dogs on Saturday.' They little know that the dirty job will just be starting. And, by god, it will be a dirty job. 'To hell with them walking over my land. How about my pheasants?' 'But, John, I can't go round in this hat. What will the neighbours think?' 'Really, Sir, don't you think you've had enough to drink tonight?' 'I tell you, gentlemen, if we hold on to this piece of land it'll bring in a couple of million cool when this slum clearance goes through.' 'I ask, electors of this borough, who are the people who keep you in servitude? Why should one class ...' 'I tell you, gentlemen, this new education is making the working class into a lot of Reds.' 'Damn Russia, Damn America ... Damn everybody. Push the boat out. I'm on board.' No, no, no, human nature doesn't change and it takes a war and physical danger to bring out the best in people.

I broke off this to go and get lunch. We had tomatoes stuffed with mince and peas, marrows and onions. Then a cake sweet so we don't do too badly, although I could always eat more than I get. I believe the test of rising from a table is whether you could still eat a hard-boiled egg. I could still eat a hard-boiled egg. Eggs, incidentally, are a glut on the market in this country. So are onions. Both are the two staple foods and one eats tons of each. Marmalade, too, from Palestine!

It's all very stupid when you think how short you are of these products. I do hope you get enough to eat.

The people here are in the main very amusing to watch. The R.A.S.C. is not like the R.H.A. as you probably know and as potential officers we are a very unsoigné lot. The big majority are putting on a badly-rehearsed act of pretending to be what they are not, but after four weeks the façade is beginning to wear a little thin and the carefully thought out elocution becomes increasingly dubious. It causes one a certain cynical and unworthy amusement but I don't greatly like people to pretend to what they're not. As always, my emotions are torn in two (I'm a Gemini child). If I stayed with the R.H.A. I would be in a crack regiment of which I had every cause to be proud, amongst men who accepted me and liked me, but amidst considerable danger and physical discomfort. In the R.A.S.C. I can feel no unit pride but it is more comfortable and very much safer. I am afraid I shall always feel my allegiance is with the R.H.A. and I shall always regard it as my regiment. Hardly any of the people here have ever heard a bullet fired in anger and those that have, only once or twice. So I am the only one who has really been on what I regard as real active service. It gives one a demoralising sense of superiority but, of course, I am careful never to talk about my experiences. Long ago, I learnt that any soldier who had never been in action hated to hear the experiences of those who had. But he always liked to pass on the other stories of the odd bomb that perchance fell on his rear H.Q. Queer thing human nature.

Well, my dear, I have written a lot to you and Leslie today. And as I have still got to write to the parents I must stop.

My dearest love, and blessings on you.

G

❧❧

Cadet Watson G. 979135
R.A.S.C. Training School, M.E.F.

September 20th, 1942

Beloved D,

Last week in replying to your 39th letter I said that 37 and 38 had not arrived. Well, lovely surprise that it was, 38 came along last week – I am hoping that 37 may yet put in a tardy appearance. Incidentally, when I wrote you I also wrote at length to Leslie about his scheme – I am telling you this just in case a tragedy happens and the letter gets lost.

I am not surprised that you find it a bit difficult to picture fighting except in terms of the cinema. In my experience at any rate, it's not like that. Sometimes I've read reports in the papers of battles I've been in and I've said to myself 'my God, was it really like that? I must have been looking at the wrong part.' Don't forget that the desert is a vast place with any amount of room for dispersion and movement. It's not like sitting in a trench in the last war where they could shell you all day long. If it gets too hot, well in nine cases out of ten you can move out to somewhere else. Don't forget, too, that with vehicles 200 yards apart it's very difficult to hit anything either from the air or on the ground. I'm not pretending warfare is like eating ice-cream but it's not so bad as one's apt to imagine. If it was, no man could stick it. And don't forget that for every hour when you have reason to be terrified you have a thousand hours with nothing to do but be bored – and I think I've seen as much fighting as ninety per cent of the people on the desert – Gubi, Sidi Rezegh, Gazala, Micheli, Antelat, Agedabia, El Agheila, El Adem, Mersa Matruh, Alam el Halfa.

Did I ever tell you of the first time I was nearly captured? It happened on the first day of the May push. I was going back to R.H.Q. from the troop and we were about five miles behind our gun position. I was sitting in front of the vehicle with the driver and our Sergeant-Major. We were in an area where the Free French were in action. As we were driving along we saw a battery of 25 pounders (English guns) drop into action about five hundred yards on our left. We watched, vaguely thinking they must be the Buckshee Frogs (Free French!) Then we saw a staff car driving towards us and so we stopped politely, thinking he must want to know where he was. He drove up to us, stopped with his car across our bonnet. We smiled a welcome. 'You are my prisoners,' said one of them, poking a rifle menacingly at our stomachs. We stared at him speechless. At last the horrible truth dawned on us. This was no Free French, they were Germans. At last our Sergeant-Major found his tongue. 'Bugger off, man, for christ's sake,' he said. 'No, no, you are my prisoners,' said the German and waved his rifle about. 'Listen, c--t,' said the Sergeant-Major, 'I said f--k off, and I meant f--k off. F--k off, can't you?' I listened to this dialogue in some anxiety (I have reported it verbatim). The German got very excited. 'Follow me,' he said, 'you are my prisoners.' 'All right, blast you, we'll follow,' said the Sergeant-Major. He leant down and whispered to the driver, 'Get cracking like a dose of salts as soon as we start,' he said. The German waved to us to follow and we started up. As soon as we got moving the driver turned away, put his foot down and we were away. The German never fired at us for some reason or other!

I was nearly captured again four days later! I was driving a vehicle up with some others that we were taking up. A big dust storm blew up. Picture my surprise when a dirty big German tank loomed out of the dust 30 yards on my right. Did we get moving! I played a tune on that gear-box that would have delighted Sir Malcolm Campbell.

Pops is very amusing in his letters. He keeps talking about the iron in my soul being tempered with true steel. I think it would be much nearer the mark to talk of the iron in my soul being changed into sand in my intestines. Still I've been amazingly lucky so far, touch wood. One day I'll become a club-bore proper and tell you all about it.

At the moment we are learning all there is to know about the petrol engine. I don't somehow picture myself maintaining the family car, for all that. So long as they go I don't much care how they go. Still, it's fairly interesting to watch the wheels go round. Apart from that I've been indulging in an orgy of bridge.

I've also been reading a very light and only moderate book called *Vinegar and Brown Paper* by John Paddy Carstairs, which is about a troup of Les Girls. It reminded, me, however very much of days – or rather nights – at the Dorchester. So that at the moment *re* our *rus v urbe* argument – my desire for rusticity and a cabbage has been replaced with a desire for lubricity and a gardenia. Roll on the revolution and all that but please leave me the Embassy, where one can behave in a manner that has rather a nasty smell about it.

I suppose that after the war I shall be one of the best-dressed men in London. While Gaga Mole goes to the Savoy tastily garbed in that little piece you've run up for him out of a bonnet cover and a couple of vests, I shall be strutting round in my new pre-war Kilgour and French. Post-war days will certainly have their moments, one way and another!

Judging by a notice just published, Christmas mail must be posted now. It seems a bit early but just in case – the very loveliest seasons greetings to you, G.M. and the Mole. There are no facilities for gifts here, but when I go on leave in Cairo I may be able to fix something up. I do wish I was in England when Mole appears. What preliminary Hell and then what lovely Heaven. I know I shall adore him even if he does drip simultaneously at three ends.

You might show the appropriate bits of this letter to the parents. They will be interested and it will save me repeating myself.

Your letters are heaven, and I look forward all the time to the post. It's no use repeating how much I miss you but when I receive your letters you seem even nearer than usual and that's saying something.

Your very devoted G

❧

Cadet G. Watson
M.E.F. O.C.T.U.

October 25th, 1942

Darlingest D,

It is three weeks since I last wrote you and they have, I think, been the funniest three weeks I have ever spent since I've been in the army. That this place would be improved by the addition of the Marx brothers, I don't deny, but it is quite sufficiently belly-aching as it is.

Let me start at the beginning. Before leaving the R.A.S.C. Training School I had forty-eight hours in Cairo. The hotels were packed and we couldn't get in anywhere. Eventually one said they would put us up in the Dining Room. I went to bed quite happily lying on top of the sheets in a very short vest and very short pants. I awoke next morning at nine to find my bed surrounded by people busy at their breakfast and apparently quite unconcerned at my phallic apparatus which, I am ashamed to say, was in a state that would not have disgraced a randy stallion. Fortunately the breakfasters were exclusively military – and possibly envied me my luck.

We came here last Thursday after an unpleasant but quite humorous railway journey of 24 hours – normally about 8. I slept on the floor of the carriage and got devoured by bugs.

Nothing that I can say about this place can possibly re-picture to you the truth. I go round in a permanent state of hardly concealed mirth that will any moment break out in the face of the instructors. The general idea appears to be that you should learn to endure discipline. There are several methods of instilling this. One is to put you on a charge every five minutes of the day. Here are some of the charges that have been laid against some of my friends (I have escaped to date): a) Coming on parade with the heels of his boots worn down. b) Standing watching a demonstration with his arms crossed. c) Dirty brass (it was simply spotless) and so on *ad infinitum*. Our rooms have to be bull-shone (not the right word, ask Leslie) to the nth degree. Ours was cleaner than I have ever before seen a room. We were called out on parade by our company C.O. 'I don't know,' he said, 'if you would even allow men to sleep in a room like that. If you did they would certainly catch dysentery. There is a latrine across the road, is it necessary for you to make another of your living quarters.' The webbing provided by the government is dark green. We have to get ours white. We discuss endlessly the rival merits of salt, Brasso, anti-gas ointment, bleaching powder, etc. The only time we aren't scrubbing is when we are polishing. We are drilled by Guards Sergeants. It is the funniest parade I have ever been on. You wander meekly onto the parade ground. Suddenly you are surrounded by a pack of baying wolves. You can't understand a word they say but you find yourself rushing round the parade ground at an incredible speed banking hard at the corners. I don't know what speed Leslie marches at, but we take steps of about four inches at about 750 to the minute: they don't give orders they shout 'wow waugh-wow-waugh' and you do something or other. If you all think of doing the same thing together it doesn't much matter what. One of my friends – slightly deaf – heard the sergeant bellow 'wow-wow wow-wow-wow-wow', which turned out to be 'move to the right in threes, right turn.' He stepped smartly out of the ranks and said, 'Here, Sergeant.' Another friend was asked his name. He thought he was being greeted with good-morning, so said, 'Good-morning, Sir.' 'Spell it,' they boomed back. As you march around the barracks, strange sergeants keep bobbing out of drains and ditches and start yelling out the step to you. The lectures, too, are very funny. Ninety-five per cent of the class knows much more about the subject than the lecturer and pandemonium reigns. Till today my feet have hardly touched the ground but now my webbing is approaching its correct whiteness so things are improving. Meanwhile one laughs and laughs and laughs and wonders whether it is really true there is a war on.

I haven't had any more letters from you since I last wrote as there is some delay in forwarding them on from the R.A.S.C. joint but I expect they will be along shortly.

Incidentally, we are now in Palestine which is a very pleasant change from Egypt. It's nice to see green fields and hills again. The oranges are just coming in!

Take care of yourself, bless you. Please remember me to G.M.

Devotedly,

G

❧

December 6th, 1942

Darling D,

It is a long time since I have written to you. I have, actually, been meaning to write for some time but I have delayed doing so in the hope that I should soon get a letter from you which I could answer. But none has, as yet, arrived and I mustn't delay any longer.

I dearly wish I could be with you now. I haven't any actual date as to when Mole is expected but you said somewhere around Christmas so I suppose he may be expected any day now. Please God it is not too awful. As to Mole – of whatever sex – he will of course, inevitably be one of the most adorable infants and I long already to make his – or her – acquaintance. But at such a time I would give anything just to be there to keep a friendly eye on your activities. God bless you.

One bit of gossip that will please you. One of my drill instructors here is in the Grenadier Guards and apparently knew Leslie quite well at the Depot. His name is Sgt. Tilson. My stock went up immediately when he found I was his brother-in-law. 'A very fine gentleman, Sir. He was one of our most popular officers.' Did I ever tell you the staff here call us 'Sir'. It makes me laugh. 'The tall gentleman with the glasses, you're marching round like a bag of dirty washing, Sir.' Somehow the Sir at the end rather takes the sting out of the rest.

I'm afraid my career here has not been the success it should have been. I've done no work at all and have found it absolutely impossible to take the place seriously. My company commander is called Straker and is a cousin, I believe, of Major Straker, of Callaly Castle[1], was it? He is a

99

very amusing person, who does his best to take this place seriously but his real views about it coincide, I believe, with mine. My final report read as follows. 'A cadet with more than average intelligence who has carefully avoided showing any of his obvious ability in his work here.' I went in to see Straker about this. 'This isn't very good, Watson.' 'No, Sir.' 'It looks to me as if you had been very lazy.' 'Yes, Sir.' 'Why haven't you done better?' 'Well, Sir, quite frankly I haven't found the course wildly exciting.' A great grin spread over his face. 'Watson,' he said, 'I am fully aware that the course is not wildly exciting, but it is your job to convince me that you find it so.' 'Then, Sir, may I apologise to you for failing to conceal from you my opinion.' 'You may,' he said. 'You'll make a very good officer. Good luck.'

Actually, one of the things in which I have been very lucky is a couple of friends I've made. They were both at R.A.S.C. Training School with me but I didn't really know them there. But here we do everything together and they have the same views about what makes them giggle and I've seldom if ever in the army been presented with so many causes for belly-aching laughter as I've had here. So together we've really had a lot of fun.

You will, I hope, forgive this pokey little letter but I want to write you an airgraph which will arrive sooner than this and I have to do a little work today for the final exam we have tomorrow. So I really must stop. I'll write you again when I am on leave.

I think of you constantly and you feel very near to me.

Lovingly G

❧

2/Lt G.A. Watson

---

[1] Pre-war Northumbrian acquaintance

R.A.S.C. Base Depot M.E.F.

December 16th, 1942

Darling D,

You have been very much in my thoughts these last few days. As I do not know the expected date of arrival I cannot even tell whether perhaps you are now already a Mother. I wish I knew. Furthermore, being on leave I shall get no post until I report, when I hope some will have been sent on from O.C.T.U. I shall anxiously await a cable and pray that you may have help and no fear in your ordeal. Dear God that I might suffer for you. Though even that is not all true because I have learnt now that suffering has a place to fulfil like happiness, and to escape the one you lose the other. I sent you a cable which I hope you got.

This letter is, in itself, an event – my first to you in my new grand capacity. My thoughts about it all are so muddled I am not trying to sort them out. One changes from R.H.A. to R.A.S.C. – what comment can one make on that? One changes from ranker to officer – what must I feel about that? *C'est la guerre,* and it is my fate. I am too wily a bird to query Master Fate any longer. Meanwhile, being human, I am enjoying my leave and the comforts my status has brought with it. It is pleasant – after two and a half years – to travel through life again first class, even though one may have hesitant doubts as to whether one has paid too much for the price of the ticket. In any event they are not doubts which worry one frequently. As to the future and what it holds for me, I shall know more in detail in a week's time and more in large when the gods decree that that particular chapter shall be written.

Yesterday we had a lovely day. We hired a car and drove down to the Dead Sea. When one stands on the Allenby

Bridge the Jordan looks like any muddy, slow-running Hampshire stream. It was a beautiful, sharp winter day with the sun shining out of a cloudless sky. There was practically no traffic and everything was very silent and very still. I leant over the bridge and stared at the water and peace filled my being.

I thought of Britford and a hot summer Sunday and the smell of the sun on the leather of the Wolseley. And then we stopped by some farm, quiet amid the ridiculous lush green meadows. And we got out and loaded ourselves with rods and books (*Passage to India*) and rugs and cushions and mackintoshes and bottles and hampers and bathing costumes and staggered through the fields to the water's edge like drunken, overloaded pack mules. Good days, those.

And then we went to that very nice hotel on the shores of the Dead Sea, and I admired the bottles in the bar – bottles I have never seen since I came out here – Bols Gin and Curaçao and Orange Bitters etc. And we had a very gay lunch and I persuaded two of the party to bathe in the Dead Sea and I laughed as the salt got in their eyes and their mouth and their nose and Laurie – who is enormously fat and jovial like an Italian ice-cream man, and beams good-will and we tease him about his size – Laurie bobbed about like a cork and cursed me soundly for making him bathe. Then we had a very good tea and I played *Star-Dust* and *Bitter-Sweet* records on a gramophone and thought of the soft feel of Ruth's[1] body. Then we drove home through the sunset and the hills were washed blue, and purple and red and gold and green and they made me think of Simonside and hot chestnuts cooking in front of the fire. Then we had a hot lazy bath and a good dinner and then we went into the town and saw a man selling hot corn-on-the-cob and he sold Laurie one two feet

---

[1] Pre-war girl friend

long and we ate them furtively down a side-street because we didn't think it right for a British officer to be seen eating corn-on-the-cob in the street! And then we went to the King David and had another dinner and I got a little drunk and I went to bed and wished a little that I had a nice soft body to share it with me. I was very happy.

You must meet Laurie – he's heaven. We call him B.B. – the Barrage Balloon – and he is a relation of Annie. Do you know Annie? It is a very sad story. Annie was another barrage balloon and the men who tended her loved her very much. Every evening she used to go up to 10,000 feet (Laurie is only allowed up to 10,000 feet when he is very good) and sail gaily about in the night sky and she was very happy and before going to sleep her crew used to look up at her and say proudly – and very tenderly – 'Good old Annie'. And then one night a tremendous thing happened. A German plane which wasn't looking ran into Annie and crashed. But so did Annie, poor Annie. And they gave the crew another balloon but they didn't know what to call her because somehow or other it didn't seem quite right to call her Annie, if you see what I mean.

Laurie gets very annoyed when we tell him he will easily get a job in civil life at a race-course (every time they go round him once they will have done a quarter of a mile). He says we are giving him a phobia about his size. Every time he comes to a door he finds himself asking himself whether he will be able to get through, or whether the chair will collapse. As he points out no chair ever has collapsed. So he went the other day to get a bath and he was lying peacefully dreaming of six Porterhouse steaks when suddenly the bath overturned and deposited him on the floor in three inches of water. I pointed out to him that I hadn't many baths over-turn when I had been in them – which seems to prove something or other. In the group photographs I sent home he is end man on the left in the back row.

Then there is James – he is standing on my left in the photo. He is six feet four and a half inches. He laughs a lot, makes some very good remarks and eats as many ices as Laurie – or I. But we aren't very sure yet whether officers should eat ices, so we eat peanuts or corn-on-the-cob instead.

Later

I am sending you a lot of photographs of me looking rather superb in my regalia. I am sending some to the parents, too, and the idea is that if one of the two letters gets lost you can give the other one the set – or have copies made of whatever you want. I suggest that they might suitably be hung in the W.C. out of reach above the toilet roll. Out of reach or your guests would find the paper very hard and glossy. 'You can always tell which is Graham, dear, he's wearing a hat.'

Last night one of the party produced some girls and we went to the King David and danced. If they were army classified they would be: girls, things little attractive. They spoke English, thank God. The previous night I had ogled a very attractive dame in a café for hours. She was obviously odd girl out in three. By the time I had decided to make a reconnaissance (as they say in the army: time spent in recce is seldom, if ever, wasted) dancing was over for the night. I sidled up to the man in the party. 'Excuse me, Sir, if I am stepping off with the wrong foot, but would mademoiselle care to come dancing with me tomorrow?' He smiled sourly. 'Mademoiselle only speaks Yiddish.' I retired somewhat abashed. My recce had obviously been imperfect. The girls last night were, thank God, very easy to entertain and although it had rather the appearance of a stenographers' outing, it was quite good fun.

I have been looking round for a suitable present for you but everything is infernally difficult. Enquiries that I have made have been rather unproductive but there are wholesale regulations e.g. parcels are not, I gather, exempt from duty; all clothes, materials, stockings etc. are subject to clothing coupons being handed in; food may not be exported; there is a maximum weight restriction of five lbs. The only things here worth while are bags, stockings etc. and as they mostly seem to be exported from England there does not seem to be much point in making them repeat the journey. I shall look round again tomorrow. Otherwise I shall wait till I can get to Cairo where there really are some nice things.

I must stop this now or no aeroplane will take the load.

My love to my very lovely sister,

G

❧

2/Lt G.A. Watson
522 Coy R.A.S.C.[1]
50 Div. M.E.F.

January 27th, 1943

Beloved D,

It was a tremendous day returning to the company and receiving Mother's laconic cable that you were a Mother and I a Godfather. I had waited, in doubt and worry, since Christmas (when you had told me Simon was expected) and it had seemed a long wait. Now I have an even longer wait before me before I can meet the gentleman personally. That he is an impossibly attractive infant I have no doubt: that he contains all the best of his exceptional Mother and Father is

---

[1] 522 Company Royal Army Service Corps

certain: that he will be the apple of his Uncle's eye goes without saying. He starts life with the tremendous advantage of his parents being pretty nice folk. I am certain he will grow to be a worthy Watson-Gault – and what more could anybody possibly desire? You must be very proud of him and I have no doubt are competing furiously with Gaga as to who can spoil him most absurdly the quickest.

I wrote to you last about a week ago and very little – other than my pleasure at writing you – has transpired that justifies another letter. I spent one night – as I sometimes have done in the past – in reading again your letters. The joy and encouragement and hope that they have brought me you will only be able vaguely to guess at. They make me feel that all this disagreeable present has some point – that there is a future worth waiting for. They make me laugh in an intimate way that nothing else does. They give me news of home from an angle of gossip such as no-one else sends me. They cheer me in my black moments and gladden me further in my best. You would be embarrassed if you knew how eagerly I wait for the familiar blue envelope. To date I have received every one in the series except 37, 41 and 44 – I have hope that the latter may still turn up. What a strange period they cover. You write, for instance, in April 1941 and wonder whether I will be home again before I have time to receive your first letter. I have been here now for practically two years! Twenty-one strange, eventful months, what stories we shall tell each other. How I shall welcome the chance of sinking into PEACEFUL oblivion. May it be soon.

One or two local Arabs in Libya have received letters from the authorities thanking them for helping our prisoners to escape from Benghazi. The other day I was approached by one of them.

'Sayida, George.' (Good-morning, you blue-bottomed old bastard.)

'Sayida, George, Yallah.' (Good-morning, you pregnant daughter of a sterile scorpion. Get the hell out of here.)

'Shufti, George, shufti.' (Take a look at this, you winkle-necked dog-fish.)

'Imshi, George, iggni.' (Get moving bloody quick, you rancid cow dropping, or you'll know why.)

'No, no, George, shufti,' and he started to undress. First he undid his pinched Itie[1] great-coat, then he undid his second pinched Itie great-coat, then he undid his English pinched great-coat. Then he lifted his dressing gown and nightdress and produced a small note-book with three pages in it which he thrust at me. Expecting the usual afore-mentioned letter, I had a look. There was only one bit of writing on it. In block capitals it read 'Beware! Here comes the man from the Maypole!' I roared with laughter. The Arab, delighted, roared with laughter. We parted excellent friends.

The weather here for the past month has been almost English. Bitterly cold and rain every day. When it does rain here it rains in very good measure. The desert is a quagmire and we go sloshing round the mud. Rather like a Point-to-Point in England when all your horses are last, you don't know any of the local gentry, there is a bitterly cutting East wind and – as ever – it is pouring.

I am afraid this is a very dull letter, but little new has happened to get my mind turning on subjects on which I can write. It comes to you, however, with my absurdly devoted love and blessings.

I miss you terribly.

G

⊷⊶

---

[1] Italian

2/Lt G.A. Watson
522 Coy R.A.S.C.
50 Div. M.E.F.

February 12th, 1943

D darling,

The weather out here is playing one strange tricks. Today the sun, with little heat, is shining out of a pale blue sky, streaked here and there with wisps of white cloud. A fresh wind is blowing and there is the threat of rain before nightfall. Meanwhile there is a glorious tang in the air – in the immortal words of Pops 'just like champagne' – and when one is out-of-doors one's cheeks glow with a healthy warming pink. In short, it is a typical English January day of the better sort. The sort of day when one went striding off to Hillhead and round home by Tosson with a dinner (sorry, lunch!) of steak and kidney pie, brussels sprouts, roast potatoes, treacle pudding and tomato soup to look forward to, followed by a peaceful sleep in front of a blazing fire, interrupted by the monotonous but fascinating snore of Peter warming his tummy at the blaze. Pops and you would stride in front discussing sex and pursued by the shouted entreaties of Mops to wait for Peter who was languidly and disinterestedly pursuing a zig-zag course of his own half a mile in the rear and quite unconcerned in the possession of the knowledge that inevitably the whole family would wait, and, that if he lingered sufficiently, he would probably be carried into the bargain. Never did Hitler rule people with such un-questioning allegiance, never did Mussolini demand such instant obedience. With Churchill he possessed a dominat-ing personality. Such is the day and it accords ill with a khaki-clad multitude fighting a war – at present very far distant – in the M.E. two thousand miles from home.

One of the officers has produced from home some copies of the *Tatler* and *Bystander*. I read them with my mouth hanging open. There was Lady Jersey – faultlessly chic – selling programmes at the premier of *Eagle Squadron*. In this good work who should she be assisted by? Why, none other – but let me quote the passage in full, 'Long office hours keep Lady Bridgett Poulett's lovely face too much hidden, but on this occasion she was among the programme-sellers, ethereal and exquisite. Mrs Charles Sweeney was another on this job; Miss Ghislaine Dresselbuys, looking very slim and starry-eyed and Princess Natasha Bagration whose appearance has special distinction'! There were photos of Countess Cadogan and her 'happy family' etc. etc. Am I screwy or is somebody else? There has, apparently, been a big stink in the press about the paper we publish in Russia showing our war effort: Rural Britain (*vide* war-scarred Caucasus); Trafalgar Square undamaged (*vide* Stalingrad) etc. Why not have done with it and distribute the *Bystander* to the Red Army. Gad, Sir, civilisation must go on, you know, up Lady Astor! However, I need hardly tell you I read it from cover to cover with a morbid enjoyment. And yet some wonder when people have the temerity to ask whether we are a united people, whether the burden of war is equally shared. What is this country I hope to return to, D?

The war news is absurdly good at present. Everybody has the unspoken hope that perhaps the year may see it through. Mr Churchill, however, speaking at the Casablanca conference, says that should Germany crack first, the full weight of our effort will be turned against Japan. This, of course, is common sense, but I must confess that personally I have small wish to fight the little yellow men after this lot is finished. Meanwhile, people are questioning why our most successful army – the 8th – should be put under the command of an American. Others are still scared stiff at the prospects of an early Russian Victory. Most expound a general dislike and distrust of the French. A united world? Gercha!

We were having a heated argument in the Mess last night. I said that the people at home were interested in the activities of their relatives in the M.E. – not their war experiences which, God knows, are boring to hear for anyone – but the actual details of what life on the desert really is. I said that till you have experienced it, it was absolutely impossible to visualise it and that the M of I[1] should make a film about our actual mode of life. A new officer just arrived from England said: 1) That Mrs Robinson was much more interested in the five brats she had to look after than in young Johnny 'in them there strange parts.' 2) That she would much rather see Robert Taylor than the 8th Army cooking over a petrol fire. 3) That till he came out here she had never heard of 8th Army, 7th Armoured Div, Jock Campbell, etc. etc. 4) That Mrs Robinson was much more interested in her own problems of rationing than that young Johnny was fighting at some strange unpronounceable place called Alamein. What do you think? Probably educated people are interested in the doings of their relatives abroad. I'm sure my family is. But what about the great mass of the people?

Later

I have just returned from a concert party of more than average ability. It contained three reasonably attractive beazels[2]. It seemed grossly incongruous to see them in their evening dresses stuck out in the middle of the desert. It must take a bit of pluck to come up here where there are only men, men and more men and no sort of civilised amenities. I raise my pip to them in admiration and respect.

------

[1] Ministry of Information
[2] Damsels

I have had a letter from Mops written since Simon arrived. He is, as I expected, a bouncing babe. But I can't get over the fact of him having six fingers. Queer the laws of heredity. I long to hear more about him from you.

The mess has filled up and writing is getting very difficult so I'll stop now but will write soon.

I miss you terribly. Good-night and I will be thinking of you as usual when I go to bed.

Devotedly,

G

❧

Rothbury

April 15th, 1943

Beloved G,

I have a sudden urge to write to you in spite of the wireless which is both an inducement and deterrent. I have come to the conclusion that a steady dose of wireless is as much a narcotic as alcohol – it deadens your critical faculties, deadens your intelligence, can stimulate your 'base passions' and becomes increasingly more of a necessity to the true addict. The wireless proved more deterrent than inducement, so I am continuing this in the garden. The sun is baking hot and Simonside is looking very austere except for the vivid green patches of young bracken. There is a beguiling smell of wallflowers and the vague summery hum of insects in the air. It seems the epitome of luxury to be sitting here with time stretching out to far horizons and nothing to do but absorb the peace and loveliness of it all. It is lovely to rest after the hectic stress of life since the Mole happened and I do feel gradually more human but I hate being so lonely in such happiness and long so much for you to be here to share it. Last night I looked out of the window and the moon was bright orange in the sky and not even an aeroplane arrived to shatter the incredible peace and loveliness of it. It reminded me of the Coronation night when pyres were set alight among the hills and we watched a fantastically large and yellow moon ride up and sail majestically over the hills.

A rumour was set in motion that Old Wogger was coming home on leave. My heart did some very acrobatic things before your cable came to quench the flame. It is useless to rage against the unfairness of keeping the 8th Army going after the terrific work they have done and one can only hope and pray that some glimmer of humanity might happen which would release them home. The news is terrific, but there is only the news of your arrival that will stir me to unqualified joy. I see the war purely in terms of how it affects you and even peace will be a mockery unless you are here.

Simon is in his pram. I can see two large and energetic feet hurtling through the air and a rather menacing pooh-hum is emerging from the depths. I have brought a temporary nanny with me as the doctor wanted me to have a complete rest. She is very good and I am most astonished and delighted that she should take such a keen interest in Simon's habits – mostly lavatorial – but I do find the perpetual discussion of them horribly boring. Perhaps I am an unnatural mother but I do find other things about him more fascinating than his daily output of stools. I am fighting an uphill battle in trying to make him a tough fresh-air boy. Mummy, Den and Nanny, all aged about sixty odd, believe in keeping him submerged under woollens and blankets. It's making me almost a crank on the subject, but I feel the only thing I can give him of value is a serviceably healthy body, and when Mops points out that she always kept us shrouded from the air and sunshine I can't help suggesting that possibly that is the reason we were all known as delicate children. There is nothing I can do about his brains which I hope will emerge adequately at the proper time but I do want him to have a nice hard and vigorous little bod. Did I tell you that he has the most enormous little man that ever happened which he pulls delightedly as it is fixed at such a convenient angle. He ought to be a delight to any bride.

I have saved several of your letters to answer until I had time for a proper letter so I will begin on them now. First of all W, written on Feb 12th. I could almost live again those family walks up to the Hillhead with Peter in attendance. Pops stopping for a chat to Mr Turnbull while we kept the sheep dogs from eating Peter up. We will do them again and it will seem that nothing has changed in spite of all the tremendous happenings that have interceded. Certainly the enormous lunch rather badly cooked will be an eternal feature of the place!

I doubt if those rides on Mrs Rufus[1] will ever be repeated – they are a lovely memory and I would love to do them again; perhaps we shall, in other places and on other machines but it won't be quite the same as Mrs Rufus. We shall watch Ullswater and the sun gleaming on the water from Grisedale Tarn before very long, perhaps.

Re the *Bystander* and *Tatler*, you ask me what sort of country this is. I don't feel a bit competent to judge and if you asked the same thing of a dozen people you would get different answers, all probably right. It is simpler to think of the nation as a collection of individuals and I think the average individual has changed damn little. The majority – even the nice ones – are out primarily for themselves and their own interests; their kindnesses and meannesses are mostly spontaneous and not thought out at all. The poor still want

---

[1] Horse from the local livery stable

to be rich and the rich still resent the thought of poverty but are slowly realising that there won't be much money for anyone after the war. The average person is still appallingly insular and regards all Americans and foreigners with suspicion as peculiar and unpleasant. There are, I am sure, a vast part of the population who are completely unaware that a war is on except as it slightly affects their stomachs by rationing. If you go to Claridges, I doubt if you would see a broken finger nail or a shabby woman. I believe bribing is rampant in the shops and I wouldn't say a spirit of self-denial is common. There are the exceptions, of course, people who are utterly splendid and make one ashamed – the few who tear up their clothing coupons to help the war effort, as opposed to those who blackmail their maids to use theirs as well as their own. The people who give up their houses exultantly for the Army to use, as opposed to those who use every wangle to keep their houses for their own unsullied use. A few people may have turned to religion, and others may be looking to the land and a simple life for happiness, but the vast majority will be as like after the war as they were before and only some miracle of wisdom will keep us from another war in twenty years' time. I think conditions for the working classes will improve a little, concessions made rather grudgingly by those who realise the inevitability of it, and received rather sullenly, but the effect of this or improved education can not be realised for another fifty years. I think we will slide gently into a more level bourgeois nation such as Sweden which has no extremes of poverty or wealth. If public schools go, I will then believe that England is really trans-forming into a new and surprising country with quite unpredictable results.

The other questions you ask in your letter are also difficult to answer. I should think the average person might answer fifty per cent of them with luck but I doubt if that would be any criterion of his interest in what is going on in the M.E.

Some people like facts, and assimilate them easily, but that is no test to the value of their knowledge. No matter how interested one was in London, I doubt if anyone could say how many raids it had suffered, how many churches have been hit or what were the casualties. You might be interested if I told you Fortnums had been demolished (it hasn't) because you know it and can visualise it, but if I told you that Barkers in Kensington had gone it would mean less to you, because there is no personal link. Personally, maps and statistics mean nothing to me and they merely obscure the human and personal interest which always keeps me enthralled.

Your letter X has still not arrived but I still hope and Y I have already replied to, as it was an Air Mail card, so the next one was Z, dated March 19th, 1943. It was a very sweet letter and I do so love to know about the people you are with. I do hope I shall meet them some day although I shall feel rather shy because they have done and seen so much compared to my rather selfish and uneventful war existence. Have you worn your corduroy trousers?

Your letter B (10/4/43) was a divine letter which arrived in a cloud of whisky fumes. The very breath of it unsettled me madly – gardenias and white satin! And all that those simple words meant, London! The boat to America, Madeira, glorious nights of heaven (if visited under slightly alcoholic conditions) – music strumming and dancing with the blood chasing through your veins. As you say, there is nothing comparable to it, other things perhaps but not that lovely, hot excitement, the feeling that one is living the story of which one had always dreamed.

Your next letter C was a very sober one with a delicious description of how the alcoholic one was inscribed – it would have been tragic if it had not been posted. Your feedies sound constant and plentiful which is excellent news. The rate of exchange seems rather against true nature but no doubt they do extremely well, if nefariously.

I love your long letters but it is nice to hear frequently so I think it is best for you to write whatever there is time for and according to your mood. Which would you prefer me to do?

Your letter D (April 4th) has just arrived. I am so glad you like the Moles photographs. Sometimes when Gaga is potting him it is very difficult to tell whether it's the Mole on the pot or 'Dad', they look so alike. I am so glad you liked the head only as I think it is heaven, but most people think it's dreadful.

I have not had a chance to see *Desert Victory* as it wasn't showing when I had a night out, but I am longing to see it and I believe it is simply terrific. Did the film or photographs in which you took part ever appear?

I think both Pops and Leslie feel that Beveridge[2] is promising a nice Utopia which will land the country into bankruptcy and do no good to anyone. Bigger pension schemes will increase the price of the article and make our export terms impossible etc. etc. It's very difficult to know how much one should be an idealist or how much a realist.

How is Mrs Bagnall[3]? She sounds a most adorable character. Your letters are a never-ending source of delight and amusement. I wish I could tell you all they have meant to me and will always be my biggest pride and joy.

I have been writing this solidly all day with intervals for food and the Mole, and now Pops has arrived and I must think of finishing it as the cramp from my seat is spreading to my brain and my hand is almost numb. I hate to stop as it's such ages since I had a really good gossip with you, but now that I am a lady of leisure I can start another almost

---

[2] Politician who produced the much-discussed Beveridge Plan on pensions

[3] The platoon pig, retained for subsequent consumption

immediately. It will make up for my previous lapses which I hated but which were rather unavoidable.

Gaga M. has just rung up to say that he has forwarded on a big letter from you to me, so I am longing for it, and it will be a good reason to begin another letter to you. When I go to bed tonight I will talk to you as usual. It is a lovely time and all the worries of the day, the little lonelinesses and depressions slip away and I feel close to you – so proud to be your sister.

Good-night, darling, and may God bring you back soon safely, again.

D

☙❧

2/Lt G.A. Watson
522 Coy R.A.S.C.
50 Div. M.E.F.

May 16th, 1943

Beloved D,

Back again in civilisation and not as pleased about it as I should be. Frankly, this country makes me sick. One returns from the 'blue' where one had planned the meals one was to eat, the drinks one was to drink and the dances one was to dance. What is the reality? You go into some restaurant which is packed to the ceiling. You find that the floor is packed with a) brilliantined, white-coated Gyppo city-slickers who have made a fortune out of the war who escort some lovely but inaccessible women; b) the local base wallahs who have got themselves established with the local Wrens, A.T.S. and nurses. You gaze enviously but unavailingly; c) a few despairing members of the fighting forces who pay for rather frowsy 'hostesses' rather than not dance at all. You can't dance, so you fight your way to the bar. You ask for a whisky and for 2/- you barely get enough to cover the bottom of the glass. After a while you can't stand the crowd any longer and you feel out of it not dancing so you decide to go and eat. You take a taxi. You ask how much at the other end. He says 5/-. You look at the meter and it says 2/6. You give him a 1/- and get followed into the restaurant by imprecations. Here, if you are lucky enough to get a table, you sit down for your chosen menu. You find it's been chosen for you. There is only *table d'hôte* – 3 courses for a controlled price of 6/-. But don't imagine that the dinner will cost you 6/-. There is 1/- for each small cup of Turkish coffee, 35/- for any drinkable wine, 2/6 for a cigar. You eat soup, *oeuf en cocotte,* what passes for sole, strawberries and cream (a dozen berries). You drink Asti-Spumanti. You find you have spent a pound. It is now 9 o'clock. So you decide to go back and see a cabaret. More crowds, more feeling out of it, the hell of a lot more drinks to try and get in the mood. You go home at eleven after watching a shoddy cabaret with a sore head and about £5 lighter in pocket than when you started. Next night you spend in the Mess.

You go shopping, and you try to buy some silk stockings to send home, £3 per pair. You beat them down to £2, maybe. You see a small bottle of Chanel No. 5. You think that's just the thing for your sister. It's £8. You know she'd be ashamed to wear it at that price. You ask for a royal Sovereign pencil, 2/- each. This, D, is the country we saved from Rommel. You see the Germans paying these prices, prices which have already doubled since the end of the Tunisian Campaign! Take other ranks. They have to walk about in pairs because otherwise they might be attacked in the streets – might be, I mean are – in the cafes they have to frequent because they are not allowed in any 'decent' joints which are Officers Only. They came down from the desert with £30 and they haven't had much to drink in months. Beer may be 2/- a glass but it's beer. They get tight. Then they are robbed of their money. The first night I had one of my men robbed of £10, one attacked by two Arabs. This, D, is the country we saved from Rommel. Now do you understand why I loathe it so much: why any man in the 8th Army would gladly fight out here for another twelve months – so long as he was fighting the Egyptians. I'm not allowed to write to the papers but if you care to put the above facts together in a letter to the *Spectator* I think it would be a good idea. They are the gospel truth and the prices quoted I can vouch for from my own personal experience.

There are, of course, compensations about being in this area: food in a restaurant at any price is a change to the same crowd in the same mess; cinemas are accessible at still moderate prices; baths, hair-cuts etc., are pleasant luxuries. But I must say I should like to get on with this damned war and get home. Two years away is an imposition anywhere but in Egypt it is too much of a good thing. However, things look brighter than they have ever done so it may not be long now.

I sent you off, via Mother, a small present – lipstick and compact. I tried to choose the right shade of lipstick. If it doesn't match you'll have to dye your hair. Hope it arrives ok.

The trouble with letter-writing out here is that not only does one have no news but nothing happens which stimulates one's thoughts along channels which would make an interesting letter. It is curious that being in the centre of the most momentous events in the history of the world one should find it so hard to find anything worth reporting. However, by now you will be used to the frantic boredom of my letters. Sometimes I think you must feel on seeing my envelope lying on the mat, 'Well, G's all right. Do I really need to wade through his letter.' But you have told me so often that you like my letters I must believe you. Certainly

119

you sometimes say your own letters are dull – but I find them all fascinating and read again and again every little detail. It is lovely how conversational you make them. It is like talking to you – or almost.

Sometimes, I'm afraid you must think I sound very browned off. I'm not really. Considering the fact that I have ceased to find this war very amusing it is surprising how very rarely I am fed up. But I use you as someone with whom I can get things off my chest. So you see the worst side, I am afraid. Army life is a very lone-world existence. I like very much the people in our mess, but one doesn't make friends – real friends – with them. One is perpetually wearing a cheerful, I-can-take-it air and when one writes letters it is pleasant to lift the mask and be completely natural and say what one really feels instead of just pretending. I suppose it is inevitable with a small circle of one sex all living together. You can't afford to get too intimate with each other or life would become too difficult.

Talking of pigs, Mrs Bagnall is flourishing like nobody's business. We bought a lot of chocolate which melted in the sun. We gave it all to her and she wolfed it all ravenously. She eats with all the concentrated greed and abandon of a Pekinese. Sometimes I scratch her back with a stick and she grunts with pleasure. She is now enormous. After she has eaten, her distended stomach is nearer the ground than her legs and she just swivels round on her navel like a top. Altogether Mrs Bagnall is a distinct acquisition to the platoon.

I went to the races yesterday and contrary to Wogger custom won – five winners out of seven. I was going on instinct which is clearly a more satisfactory method than form. As it meant taking money from the locals it was doubly satisfying. I have also seen two films this week: *Shadow of the Thin Man* and Monty Woolley in *Pied Piper*, which was utterly delightful. Tomorrow I am going to see Miss Hayworth and

Fred Astaire in *You Were Never Lovelier* which I look forward to. I shall swim in the pool at the Sporting Club before I go, in a rather dandy pair of swimming shorts I have bought. I suppose I mustn't complain.

My reading, of late, has been confined to George du Maurier's *Trilby* which I enjoyed although the hero was an unutterable Victorian prig. I have read a lot of books out here that I would never have read otherwise. Soon I hope to be reading Hazel's.[1]

Please convey my respects to Mole, my affection to Gaga. I think of you daily and wonder what you are doing and whether you are happy and well. There will be a letter from you shortly. I miss you terribly.

Your devoted G.

৵৩৩

2/Lt G.A. Watson
522 Coy R.A.S.C.
50 Div. M.E.F.

May 26th, 1943

Beloved D,

I have just returned from leave to find your letter-card of May 11th (no. 55) waiting for me. I would love to have been with you all at Whitton. With the Mole there I can imagine the pandemonium must have been almost pre-war. Poor Den, I know just what you mean but I have no doubt that Simon's appeal won her over.

---

[1] *Green Hands* (Faber), her humorous account of her time in the Land Army

I spent most of my leave – three days – with the Phillipses. They are fundamentally unchanged. Except that the war has improved them financially it has entirely passed them by. They live in a city where rationing does not exist and the luxuries of pre-war days are all obtainable at a price. I think that probably they are enjoying themselves as much as in pre-war days. They mingle with the Cairo intelligentsia – all the young men and women who help the war by lecturing to the Egyptians for the British Council on the Importance of Renaissance Poetry, the Danger of the Bolweevil, etc; who write un-understandable poetry which they publish at their own expense in very high-brow magazines 'designed to fulfill the need of expression of the man in the forces', which not one man in a million in the forces could hope to understand.

None of the women I met struck me as having any physical attributes although some of them were quite intelligent and amusing. I doubt whether they would have had any sexual success in England and they were no doubt glad that world conflict had put them on the map. I suppose if I were living in Cairo I would behave in very much the same way but I am not and I am jealous of those who are having an easier war than I am – and the whole thing made me slightly sick. I know how stupid it is to feel bitter. The toss of the coin decided whether you spend your time driving a tram in Blackburn, sitting on a search-light in the Hebrides, or living in the desert. But human nature is – I need hardly tell you – a curious compound and most of us out here do feel envious of those who have had an easy war. Don't for a moment imagine that this includes anyone who stuck the blitz, or civilians in general – excluding the young shirkers in the safe jobs, black marketeers etc. Nor anyone in the army too old for service abroad (Gaga) or too young, or A-A gunners. But the army who exercise on Salisbury Plain, it's not at all their fault but the price they pay is allowing us the luxury of a good grumble. We don't mean any harm, but there you are. As for your Londoners! I've just been reading Quentin Reynold's *Only the Stars are Neutral,* a fine book. I entirely agree with him that the civilians of Britain, and especially London, have won the war for us. No words can possibly express my humble admiration at your courage in sticking that blitz. Only the knowledge that the Germans are getting it back three-fold gives me any consolation. You were superb, D darling, in sticking it and I am very proud of you. What I have had to suffer in comparable danger was trifling even if the hardships of desert discomfort were disagreeable – but they, too, had their compensations and were always easily endurable. I trust we have now seen the last of the desert. I am afraid there will be a big price to pay yet before it is all over (excuse all these mistakes but the wireless is blaring out in the Mess).

For myself I look to the future, happy and confident whatever it may bring forth for me. I have no past regrets. My life with you and the family has given me a richness and happiness denied to most.

I bought a few books in Cairo – a mixed bag: *Orlando* by Virginia Woolf, *The Voyage* by Charles Morgan, *Nicholas Nickleby* (Dickens), a Peter Cheyney (the best crime story writer and the most amusing), and Quentin Reynold's book.

While we've been resting and refitting recently there has been a certain amount of re-organisation of personnel: promotions and so on.

While on leave I saw four pictures: Hitchcock's *Saboteur* (excellent, did you know how much Priscilla Lane resembles Ginger Rogers), *Desert Victory* (excellent. I'm glad I missed that battle though of course you see the worst of weeks all concentrated into a few minutes), *The Magnificent Ambersons,* (excellent, a rather arty picture directed by Orson Welles), and *You Were Never Lovelier* (Fred Astaire and Rita Hayworth, the latter looking very voluptuous. I was a little disillusioned when my companion told me that somebody else had to sing for her. Anyway she isn't a patch on Ginger). It's very nice to see films again after so long a break. Altogether I had quite a pleasant three days.

The weather here is quite agreeable just now – nice for bathing – although it is daily getting hotter. The Phillipses want to settle in Cairo after the war. They like the climate so! As an alternative they are considering Brazil! They say the flies in Northumberland are worse than out here. If they are I can only say I never noticed them. Anyhow, I think I'll take the risk. As for the climate, an east wind and biting rain sound to me like heaven. I don't think it'll be long now before we are all home.

I have, I am afraid, very little news for you and this is, as usual a very dull letter. However it comes to you with my devoted love and blessings.

G

❦

Lieut G.A. Watson
522 Coy R.A.S.C.
50 Div. M.E.F.

June 17th, 1943

Beloved D,

I wrote you a letter-card a few days ago and at the present rate mails are taking it will probably be months before this reaches you, however ... I also sent you a few days ago four pairs of silk stockings which went off separately in four separate registered letters. Let me know if they all reach you. I hope they are the right shade and size. They are in three different qualities and I hope will be useful for morning, afternoon and evening wear! I should have liked them all to be of the pure silk type but they really are a rather chronic price! True profiteering as they know that most soldiers like sending them home, so it's easy money. I love this country!

I went the other day to see Fred Astaire in *You Were Never Lovelier*. It brought back the most amazingly vivid memories of a part of my London life I hadn't thought about for some time. Essex Street, Ivor[1] getting up from his desk and, with that charming smile of his, putting on his black Anthony Eden hat, his blue silk scarf and blue overcoat; Alan, looking slightly gross in the same garb; Bernard in brown herring-bone coat and trilby. Then across to the pub to see Eva and drink a lot of sherry and gossip at all the fabulous fortunes awaiting us round the corner. Then to dinner at the Reform or the Savoy (preferably the more expensive) and then to the Tivoli in the Strand to see Eddie Cantor in *Roman Scandals* or Fred Astaire in *Gay Divine* at the Carlton or Charlie Chaplin in *City Lights* at the Tottenham Court Road – anything with lots of girls and swirling stages and broad comedy and Ivor's gorgeous laugh ringing out round the theatre. It was good fun and somehow, in essence, Astaire's new film seemed to be eight years old – in the same captivating tunes, the same haunting dances. Good days and an easy way of forgetting the very thin ice on which we were all skating at the time. Britain was, I think, decadent before the war but the people who set the fashion for the time were, I am sure, conscious of the fact that the world was sliding inevitably into a landslide that was beyond the stopping of man. With no stability, with no future, eat drink and be merry is not only the inevitable slogan but the only sane slogan. This war, to many people has been made infinitely more endurable because of the memory of years of pleasure behind them. It did not prevent

---

[1] The address of Nicholson & Wason, of which Ivor Nicholson was Chairman

them getting on with the job once the landslip had taken hold of them.

'My candle burns at both ends, it will not last the night, but oh my friends and oh my foes it gives a lovely light.' 'Safe upon the solid rock the ugly houses stand, come and see my shining castle built upon the sand.' *Vale* 1930s. We shall, I am sure, come to regard this decade with all the nostalgia we used to attach to the Edwardians. Nostalgia is a curious thing. I am already beginning to sentimentalise about the desert. Yes, I am! Those were the days! The guns ploughing across the desert, two hundred yards between vehicles, like a great convoy at sea; sitting beside one's truck at night gossiping, and, when we had it, drinking beer; making chappaties with flour and water over a petrol fire and in a converted petrol tin; frying sausages at an O.P. within sight of the enemy and not giving it a thought; the desert before Alamein, when war was only serious by short starts and for months was only a game when neither side did much damage to each other. I know, of course, that I have never hated life so much before but memory sentimentalises everything and already I am beginning to romanticise it. When I come home and tell you what a lovely time we all had, please don't believe me. On the other hand war as I have seen it up to June 17th 1943 is not comparably as bad as I thought it. Most of the time one is unutterably bored, part of the time one has no emotions at all. Sometimes one is very frightened, now and again one has real fun. But very seldom indeed is one either unhappy or miserable. Films and books romanticise and exaggerate the horrors as much as my memory is sentimentalising it. You, with your experience of the London blitz would probably agree with me after reading some of the books written about it. Still it's all bloody horrible.

I am reading Virginia Woolf's *Orlando* at the moment. It has just been published as one of the first six books published in Cairo for the troops by Penguin. It seems a curious choice – or else the army is more highbrow than I imagined.

I bathe two or three times a week[2] and you should see the élan with which I dive into the waves and even swim under water. I haven't yet tried diving into a swimming bath and have a suspicion I might belly-flop. Still I am improving daily. In this period of calm before, I suppose, the great storm there is not a great deal to do and the time hangs a bit heavily. The attractions of the city begin to pall although there is a very nice officers' club where the food is excellent and the comforts and amenities almost Pall Mallish. I spend most of the mornings busy with my platoon, the afternoons in bathing or sleep. The only trouble with the latter is that one feels so hellish waking up. It gets very hot in one's tent. In the evenings if I do not go out I stay in the mess where I drink in moderation, write letters or read. All the time the wireless, as now, is blaring out. I am usually in bed by ten. When on active service I am usually in bed by nine – sometimes by eight, when I was in the ranks, sometimes in the winter, by seven. There was nothing else to do and in the gunners we had no lights in our trucks as I have now in mine, or in the mess. The result after the war will be disastrous and Popsyish. I can see myself watching the clock and the moment it strikes ten, away I'll be. How intolerable for my wife, particularly if she's a young poppet who wants to be out till five in the morning every night. I'm afraid I've sown any wild oats I'm ever going to sow.

Did you see, incidentally, by my letter headings that I've now got another pip. No credit to me – it comes almost automatically after six months. I'm afraid I won't get any further. Promotion in the R.A.S.C. is not fast – which is the penalty – thank God – for being in a comparatively safe arm.

They've now started telling dirty stories in the mess – they

[2] On the beaches just outside Alexandria

don't often, thank God – but it makes letter writing peculiarly difficult.

Will you tell me, incidentally, in your next letter how mine are reaching you. I expect these air-mail letters take much longer to arrive than the letter-cards, but they do have the advantage that you can take your coat off, put your feet on the mantelpiece and write leisurely of anything that occurs to you without being constrained by problems of space. However, even with unlimited space I've had my say for tonight. The mess is not conducive to thought. So I'll bid you a very happy good-night with sweet dreams of Simon and Gaga. Good-night, beloved D, I miss you very much.

Devotedly,

G

☙❧

London, NW8

June 22nd, 1943

Beloved G,

Ever since I returned from the North I have had an urge to talk to you, even in this limited form, but there have been various difficulties. Apart from being endlessly busy both maternally and otherwise, I have spent most of my days in a state of semi-coma, as the Mole takes a poor view of sleep either for himself or for me. Being a creature of settled habits I can't adjust myself to being woken every hour or so for a gossip with Mole and I face each day practically unconscious except for the feeling of grit in my eyes and a head like a suet pudding. Like a bird under a weight of feathers my normal desires and emotions stir and flutter unavailingly beneath the load of suet pudding but to crystallise one's thoughts on to paper seemed an unattainable feat.

During this time I have received from you a glorious spate of letters. I long for a few hours of uninterrupted quiet in which to answer them as it would be completely inadequate to attempt a reply in one of these letter forms, whose very limitations are like prison walls which keep you strictly confined and discourage any wandering or irrelevant thoughts. At last I must bring myself to the momentous event of which I dare scarcely whisper. '4 PAIRS OF SILK STOCKINGS–' Oh, G, my darling, don't tell me you paid such an iniquitous prices as £3 a pair – heaven itself (and heaven they certainly are!) should not be bought at such a cost! Breathlessly I found four bulging packages waiting for me, all addressed in the well-known and dearly loved Wogger writing. Feverishly I opened them one by one and hastily put them down quite unable to bear so much. After the first dizzy madness had slightly evaporated I drew each pair reverently out of the envelope and my heart somersaulted at the sight. I can't possibly explain all that they mean; they are not only divine silk stockings to dazzle the eyes of a starved female reduced to the coarsest and most shapeless cotton, which make fat legs stupendous pillars for mockery and the smartest outfit grotesque, but they are a symbol of your love which is something so precious that I could keep them for ever unworn, stowed away in a drawer with the thought of them so warm in my heart that even the pillars for mockery could be regarded with foolish happiness. Does this sound fantastic sentimentality? Perhaps it is but war does odd things to one's emotions and unendurable absence makes one's heart so full of longing that even an extra drop of feeling causes an overflow which brings tears of happiness and sorrow too near to the surface. The happiness will only be

129

complete on the night you come to take me out, and the silken legs will become a riotous hyperbole and the sorrow will be nothing but a grim memory.

I have so much to tell you but it must all wait for a more opportune moment. All of it is trifling and only important because it gives me something to talk about and an excuse for writing endless nonsense because that is our only way of slightly appeasing my longing for you to be here. I think perhaps for us both we have reached a phase when the war and all it means can scarcely be tolerated and our longing for the end of it has grown almost too great to be borne. We are on the last lap and nearing home.

My dearest love and deepest thanks.

D

≪✧≫

London, NW8

June 27th, 1943

Very darling G,

I sent you off a letter-card this week telling you that I had received a lovely pile of letters from you which I was hoping to answer and now there seems an opportune moment with Gaga on duty and the Mole in bed.

I have already told you how enchanted I am with your lovely present of stockings – I feel rather a gold digger to have asked for them and would never have dreamed of doing so if I had known the price of them! I am eagerly looking forward to your other parcel which you say is on the way but has not yet arrived – anything that comes from you is exciting whatever it is and quite apart from its own value.

Your first letter was E, dated May 5th. I am very envious of your bathing though no doubt you would gladly exchange it for some of the amenities of England. I long for the sea but it is very tantalising to see it behind a hedge of barbed wire and even the chill of North Sea waters would seem seductive. We are going to Scotland again for our next leave and hope to get a glimpse of it then, but as there were no rooms free at Crinan we are having to try a new place which may be further inland than it appears on the map. A place called Kilmelford (south of Oban) – do you know it? I have not yet had a chance to send Gaga to be photographed but I will enclose some snapshots which Den took and which include some rather good ones of Mole Senior and Junior.

I am very thrilled about your rise to a full Lieutenant. If the war goes on much longer, you and Gaga will end as complete Blimp colonels and then I shall laugh like anything!

Your letter F was dated May 16th and you sounded definitely browned off. It sounds a perfectly filthy country and it is appalling to think that the reward for saving it from Rommel should be such abominable treatment of our men who did the fighting. It makes me feel so hot and angry I can't bear to think about it, as it only makes you realise all the more how unfair and futile life can be. I feel the same when I read about the sufferings of the occupied countries – a hopelessness that life can be like that and that people are still so utterly uncivilised in any of the real decencies to one another. Actually your description of a night out and what it cost is not so unlike London now. Prices are grotesque but the people who live in hired cars seem to have plenty of money to pay for anything. I tried to buy a pair of navy blue shoes and after trying ten shops in the rain eventually found a ghastly pair for which I had to give 5 coupons and paid 93/-! Until the price control they had previously been priced at 6gns.! A maternity dress which I have had being altered since March was finally stolen last week when somebody pinched the whole van while the driver was leaving a parcel at a block of flats. No doubt I shall find it being sold at one of the expensive and supposedly reputable shops for a cut rate on coupons. Incidentally, I am glad you didn't buy Chanel at £8 a bottle – I certainly would have been embarrassed to wear it at such a price. I will try and compose a letter, as you suggest, about it all but I don't want to write one that would discredit the subject and until our leave I won't get much time for writing anything really vitriolic!

You don't need to worry that you have ever written a dull or boring word to me. Your letters are living and make it possible for me to catch a glimpse of your life and yourself which is utterly precious. I am becoming an absolute addict and become as restless as any drug fiend if I don't hear from you for some time. Incidentally, your last letters have all been opened by the censors but nothing has been deleted, thank heaven! I am glad you do grumble to me if you feel like it but you don't ever seem to. I tell you all my most trivial and rather squalid thoughts and complaints and it always makes me ashamed because your letters are always so amusing and uncomplaining. I share your views on world reconstruction after the war – I want to forget this world and live life sanely and undisturbed among fascinating people like your Mrs Bagnall. I am so glad she is still with you. If you arrive with her in London we will give her a big welcome and she shall have the best bedroom and linen and lots of feedies.

Your flicks sound very up to date. They seem to reach you about the same time as we get them. I remember reading *Trilby* and being very impressed by it. It is a pleasant period to escape to just now from the reality of today. I missed *The Magnificent Ambersons*, which I had wanted to see. I'm sorry if I sound a little odd but it is a mixture of gin and hurties – mostly gin.

Your next letter was written on your birthday. I know how you feel about wasting your precious years in Egypt as youth is such a lovely and exciting time. I was thinking today that in another 16 years I shall have reached half a century! I am champing to begin life before I am too old and mentally and physically too stiff to do it! My youth has been a lovely *hors d'oeuvre*; a taste of everything, including happiness, unhappiness and plenty of excitement and pleasure. It makes a terribly good beginning but unless there is something more solid to follow I should feel very hungry at the end of the meal. My real job of creating a home for a husband and children, of accumulating interests and responsibilities, has not yet begun and unless it does soon I shall be too old to do it and my appetite will go. Life has given me so much but I haven't begun to use any of the knowledge which I have learnt. At present my life is a mechanical routine of existence without any depths of purpose and every precious day goes by with the feeling of nothing being accomplished except a few hours nearer to the end of the war. Your life, too, is still at the first course and it is better to linger over it, so that when the meal is ended you have no regrets that you were so greedy for the entrée that you missed all the earlier bits, but it's time, too, for you to begin on more solid and satisfying fare. People who marry in their early twenties skip all the earlier delights and have to eat roast beef all their life which must become very boring and bad for the digestion. Of two evils I think it is better to have too much *hors d'oeuvre* than none at all! Because you have had so much more to bear in the war than I have you will have got much more out of it on the credit side. I don't think I have gained anything from it except grey hairs! I must try and get *The Voyage* to read when we go on leave. I will get *Sparkenbroke* for you and also *The Fountain* (in case you have not read it) and also Douglas Reed's latest. I haven't read it, but I don't read much as there always seems to be chores to be done – an endless cavalcade of washing, ironing and mending. I hate doing them so much they take twice as long!

These are all the letters which I have had recently – a lovely lot which made red letter days when they came. (Why is it red letter? I thought that was something discreditable at the bank.)

I hated leaving Rothbury although it was lovely to come back to Gaga M. The Mole was so spoiled in the North, I had a very strenuous time trying to instill some discipline, and a lot of sleepless nights. He is strangely like the pre-natal Mole of my imagination – a rather bossy person with very decided views on life and some very endearing ways. He mimics everything I do which is most difficult. I had a disgusting cough which he delighted in copying on a harsh note like a corncrake. Then he produced an imitation of one of my more imbecile expressions and whenever he saw me he flung back his head with his eyes half shut and his mouth wide open looking rather arch and very absurd. When I told Hazel he did this he turned very pink and burst into tears and hasn't done it since, which made me feel awful! He is very proud of a gurgle he makes at the back of his throat and tonight we held a long conversation together which must have sounded like a couple of amorous aeroplanes. Nanny stayed on for a few days so Leslie and I took the chance of going gay. We tried in vain to get seats for Noel Coward and ended by going to *Heartbreak House* which was delightful but not one of Shaw's best. We went on to the Dorchester and had dinner consisting of soup, smoked salmon and vegetables as a *main course* and a *savoury*. Two women were dancing together and I couldn't help wondering what you would think of it all. It closed down at mid-night and we couldn't get a taxi and had to walk all the way to St. John's Wood. There is something different in walking home because you are young and in love and the night is enchanted, to walking home in light shoes because there is no alternative!

I think I am to blame mostly as people find me madly

boring and are always criticising Leslie and me for leading such dull lives. I think it's a reaction we are suffering from all those years of living at an emotional pitch, followed by the war and the strain of the blitz. I have been horribly conscious of it since Simon was born; a feeling of being mentally, emotionally and physically spent: a sense of complete disintegration which makes me feel a stranger to myself and to everyone else. I find I can't talk to people – I seem to be shut off in a world which is like a marathon jitterbug where one goes on moving because one can't stop. (The sirens have just gone.) I began to feel better at Rothbury and found Mops' undemanding unemotionalism a perfect rest, but I wasn't there long enough for the effect to last. I am telling you this partly because it is easier to clarify one's thoughts and, if you have found a difference in my letters, you will understand about it. I am not unhappy or ill but rather in a stupor, but it won't last for ever. Pops has been sending me a spate of literature extolling the virtues of poverty. Having married a man who is self-supporting Pops feels it is his duty to remind me that 'money is not all.' I can't think of anything more destroying. Bugger poverty as far as I am concerned. Poverty means tiredness, and dirt and anxiety and none of the graces of life. I am leading the life of a poor woman now as war has reduced everyone to the living level of poverty, and I repeat, bugger poverty. I love beautiful things, I love leisure, I love good living and none of Pops' pamphlets can alter that. Actually, poverty affects a woman much more than a man. A man only works so many hours a day, whether he is a manual labourer or an industrial king, whereas the work of a poor woman is never done; she has no Saturday or Sunday from her job and no holiday in the year. No, I don't fool myself that poverty is life and it seems as silly to laud it as it is to laud money for its own sake.

Sorry about all this. It must be the surreptitious influence of the curse – mostly gin.

135

I could go on for pages yet but there won't be a chance for a day or two so I will post this and continue in another letter.

I awoke this morning feeling very Mondayish after a disjointed night with Mole. You can imagine my joy when I found a letter from you at breakfast as I had imagined that I would not be hearing from you for some time having had so many. It was T written on June 16th and I loved every word of it and have romped through my morning's work with a much lighter heart. I will answer it in detail in my next letter.

Oh my beloved G, how sick I am of this war and being without you for so long. You feel so close to me in spite of the years you have been gone and the distance that separates us but I long to be able to see you and to know that you are safe and at home.

Very lovingly,

D

&

Lieut G.A. Watson,
522 Coy R.A.S.C. M.E.F.

July 15th, 1943

Beloved D,

I haven't written you a proper letter for some time so I'll try and settle down and do my best although the wireless, inevitably, does not help composition (although there are some rather tummy-turning tunes on!) and life at the moment provides little to write about. When I look back on my two years of correspondence with you I can, looking at it dispassionately, only assume that I have bored you stiff. I know, of course, that this is not the case because what you say

136

is, perhaps, one of the least important factors of a letter but for two years the stream of my inspiration has been drawn from what is essentially the same turgid spring. To pursue the simile, they flow muddy and sluggish as a Hampshire chalk stream rather than, as yours do (I'm not kidding!) like a mountain torrent chattering, murmuring and bubbling as it races through the countryside.

While writing the above I have had a background of Vera Lynn – the Forces' Favourite! I've no doubt that the accession to power of Miss Lynn proves something or other. I, as you know, like the slinky gardenia tune which makes one want to weep with nostalgia. I am a warm supporter of the crooner. But Miss Lynn has qualities which escape me. Can it be that your wonderboy is getting old? I suspect it and look anxiously in the glass for signs of decay ... Since my last birthday I feel my age. As Father, bless him, wrote on the occasion, 'So you are now twenty-eight. Another chapter closed. You are leaving the years of youth behind you and entering an era of promise and responsibility.' I'm glad of that because I've been there two years now.

After six weeks of snuffling and scratching round the farmyard that is what passes for Society on the Mediterranean Littoral, I have found an orchid growing on the dung-hill. She is a Palestine A.T.S. whom I picked up at the races. I can imagine your reaction to this: poor, sex-starved Graham has been hooked by a ghastly tart. Well, I admit I am sex-starved, but I am a long way from losing my powers of discrimination. Girls are two a penny in this joint but I've left them all alone waiting for the right one. And I found her. She is intelligent – she speaks eleven languages including Czech, Polish, Russian and Arabic. She has wit – she lived in Vienna when Vienna was a name to conjure with for sophistication and romance. She has poise – she can make her uniform look like a Mainbocher creation. She has a very pretty face – I shall prove it with a photograph when I have some to spare. She has a figure – I know. She is twenty-five and while being very innocent – she was quite upset when I picked her up – she has quite enough experience to play me like some poor netted fish. I am, I am afraid, in the very greatest danger of falling for her in a big way. I am glad to say the lady is not indifferent to my crusty charm. It is, you will say, a fearful waste of emotion for someone who is bound to move on elsewhere soon. Well, you would be wrong. I feel more human already and I know it's done me a lot of good. I had been too long without a woman to admire and take out, and give costly, silly presents to, and be proud of. Because I can assure you she is a woman any man would be proud of. You should see the envious looks I get in restaurants from those with those appalling civilians. She is called Stella Divinska. She has a Russian (White) father and a Viennese mother. She was born in Stettin and has lived in Vienna and Cracow. She had a lot of money, swims and dances divinely – rides and skis, so she says, even better. I know, of course, that nothing can come of it and that nothing should come of it. Probably I shall only be able to see her a couple of dozen times. Meantime she is a swell kid and I am very lucky. It was worth waiting the six weeks. I know, D, you would like her and you will get some idea of her from her photos.

She was at the races looking round laughingly and impudent. I thought she was waiting to be collected and fell for her straight away, so I brassed down and asked her to dinner. She was visibly shaken, but the rusty Wogger technique won the day and she came. Since then I've never looked back i.e. six days ago! I haven't been in love with anybody for four years (though I was perilously near it in Jerusalem last leave at Christmas). It's good to feel again that wonderful pot-pourri of happiness, anticipation, doubt – and realisation. On Saturday we are going to the races and then out dancing. On Sunday bathing, to Coward's *In Which We Serve*, and then dinner. Quite a good weekend for wartime?

She works in the office for Officers' Accounts as a secretary. They won't use her languages as an interpreter or anything, because she is not English. As she says, how many English can speak eleven languages including Polish, Russian and Czech. Her English is heavenly; very fluent but with a lovely Danielle Darieux broken accent. However, enough of Miss Divinska. Perhaps it's not quite enough – after all I might as well write about her as anything. I can't spare you a photo just yet so I'll try and describe her. She is petite – small as or smaller than Willie. She has long, shapely legs and a nicely rounded, smackable bot, a tiny waist, round, firm, well-developed points of interest, long tapering fingers with almond-shaped nails on an absurd little hand. A strong little chin, full lips and pearl white teeth in a mouth that never stops smiling – a nose like yours and completely wicked eyes and arched eyebrows unplucked, a big forehead and a mass of hair your colour and done the way you do it. This is a very lame description but I have just been comparing your photo with hers and in many ways you are very much alike. What more could one ask for than a small edition of sister D?

By this time, of course, you are crying with boredom. Will this man never stop talking about his girl? Well, I'll try. From the sublime to the ridiculous. I am enclosing a photo taken on the beach. Actually, the bathing here is lovely and as I have already told you I'm becoming a strong performer.

I have read quite a few good books lately. Richard Hillary's *Last Enemy*. I loved it, seems a shame that he had to end in the way he did. His conclusions are, of course, very personal. For himself they were the right solution but they are largely a matter of faith. However, one may agree with their logical basis. Thus I can quite understand him feeling as he did after digging out that woman. For myself I have not had such an experience. Thus, I loathe the Germans, what they have done and all they stand for. But I don't loathe them personally and passionately as, for instance, I loathe the

Egyptians. Because nearly all I hate about the Germans comes to me second-hand, via my intellect. I can't feel passionate hatred at a man miles away who fires a gun at me. I merely feel hatred without it being fanatical. Whereas the Egyptians I have experienced at first hand and there my hatred is fanatical. It's a bit hard to explain but it's really the difference between fanatical hatred and logical hatred – one being emotional and the other intellectual. If, for example, anything were to happen to one of those I loved then my hatred *would* become fanatical. I don't agree with Hillary either that the post-war holds out much hope.

Then I read Graham Greene's *England Made Me.* I love his books and he is a fine writer but I do wish he would get away from his almost pathological pre-occupation with the seedy – seedy is the *mot juste.* It is apparent in every one of his books I have read and I think seediness – as opposed to honest dirt, squalor or poverty – plays a smaller part in life than he makes out.

The other two books were George A. Birmingham's *Daphne's Fishing* – a frivolous below-standard trifle – and *Reaching For the Stars,* which I think is grossly over-rated. At the moment I am busy on A.G. Street's *Gentleman of the Party.*

Well, darling D. I've rambled on enough and it's time to go to bed. I hope that this week may yet bring a letter from you. What I would give to be with you again if even for a little. Bless you and keep yourself safe and well.

Devotedly,

G

140

Lieut G.A. Watson,
522 Coy R.A.S.C. M.E.F.

July 29th, 1943

D darling,

I write this from Sicily which, a casual glance at the map will confirm, is about half-way from Egypt to England. Although this is an agreeable thought it doesn't help greatly, as there is still quite a lot of the opposition between us and the home-country. However, it is undeniably pleasant to be back in Europe and out of the hated M.E. I did not come on the assault but walked ashore along a gangplank some days later with all the peace and efficiency of a port that might have been in our hands for months rather than days. We arrived after a completely uneventful voyage undertaken under the motherly eye of escorting warships. They do these things extremely well.

Needless to say my only regret at leaving was centred round the person of Miss Divinska. I wrote you in my last letter of a planned weekend. Only fifty percent eventuated. Indeed, I left within a week of meeting, which possibly was a good thing because if I had stayed longer the work of time, the great healer, might have been more complicated than in fact has proved to be the case. Here one's previous existence seems so impossibly remote that only occasionally does one feel a faint tinge of heart's ease. She was, however, a very swell person. I enclose two photos which, needless to say do not in any way do her justice. They were taken and developed in one motion by one of those perambulating camera men. However, they will give you a remote idea of the attraction of the general article. However, that chapter, sweet as it was, is now closed.

There is little I can say about Sicily. You will have read enough about Southern Italy to have a clearly formed picture in your mind of the country I am in. Hills rising up into the centre of the island, winding, dusty, narrow roads, little villages perched on the hillside, olive, orange, almond orchards, fields of tomatoes, vines, corn-on-the-cob and melons. At the moment all the above mentioned goodies are in season and very good they are. I have already given myself tummy ache by eating too much fruit. It's very lovely up in the hills and quite unspoiled. I went up there for a run yesterday. At the moment we are encamped in an almond orchard – nearby there is a little stream and we have found a pool in it about four foot deep and fifteen yards long. I try to bathe there once a day. It is very peaceful and in some ways reminiscent of the Coquet round about Holystone. Except for the water which is lovely and warm. The principal reminder of war is the constant stream of our planes which seem to fly at will wherever they wish. The inhabitants are fantastically friendly and it is difficult to remember they are our enemies. You drive up to a farm to get eggs. They look at you suspiciously and then you say, *Buon Giorno*. Immediately, wreathed in smiles, they cluster round your car, cracking almonds for you or peeling prickly pears – anything to show willingness. I cannot quite understand this, unless it is that they are so near to the soil that the war means nothing to them. Would Procter behave the same with Germans? I doubt it and hope not. But then, perhaps, the Germans behave rather differently to us. As one farmer said: 'The Italians and Germans just took what they wanted. You English ask and then pay.' I wish I had learnt more Italian at Rapallo that time.

Best crack of the month just taken from the personal column of the *Universe*: 'Single man, 52 years old, no experience, wants light work at a convent.' I vouch for the truth of this.

Even in a comparative Eden like this place there is inevitably a toad-in-the-hole. The mosquitoes at night are simply impossible and after dusk one must either live under a mosquito net – or, if out – cover yourself in cream. It is a very malarial district. During the day one is inevitably pestered by flies – not as bad as the desert, but bloody awful just the same. Other fauna are snakes, beautiful crimson dragonflies which play about the water of our swimming pool – and a rather attractive black butterfly. It is very pleasant and peaceful in the cool of the evening to walk along the banks of the stream as it winds down a deep gorge.

I am writing this under some discomfort which probably makes the writing even more illegible than usual. I am perched on a high chair from an abandoned house, sitting under an almond tree, with the pad perched on my knee and flies nibbling the bare flesh of my arms and knees. A slight breeze is pleasant from the heat point of view, but is rather apt to blow the paper about.

I am afraid my brain is rather sterile at the moment. I should, by rights, have heaps to write about coming to a new theatre of war but in fact I find I have very little to say. At the moment a diversion has arrived: a very sweet old peasant woman who is sitting at my feet skinning almonds for me. I say, '*Grazie, multo buono,*' which is about as far as I get. It makes letter-writing even harder than it would be if I only had an empty brain to cope with.

I've been having rather a spate of agricultural books of late. *Lonely Plough*, A.G. Street's *Gentleman of the Party* and Adrian Bell's *Silver Ley*. Quite fun, but I don't somehow see myself becoming a farmer.

I haven't, of course, had any letters for some time but I expect the post will be catching up with us before long. I long for another letter from you – something always seems very wrong when I don't hear from you for sometime.

I must cease this rustic nonsense. I'll write again soon when my brain is less sterile. Till then, beloved D, my dearest love and blessings.

Devotedly,

G

❧

Very beloved G,

Having written the address and date of this yesterday I got no further. I was intending to answer, among others, your lovely long letter L (July 15th) which arrived on Saturday and now today another heavenly letter came, M (July 29th).

In your letter L you tell me all about meeting Stella Divinska. She sounded such an enchanting person and I was so glad that you had found somebody to make you happy and to make life more tolerable. I admit that I suffered the usual doubts and fears of the unknown. I wonder why one should be so insular and such a ready prey to fear, especially for those one loves. I have heard that fear is one of the deadly sins and I suppose it is such complete negation of faith. I think I understand why people are jealous of lovers: to be in love is such an intoxication. You leave everyone and everything behind and enter an incredible world where no-one can follow you: you lose your identity and all your defences, and are in a state of complete vulnerability. Those who love you stand by helplessly, knowing that you have slipped away from them, knowing that you may be hurt but they can't share it; knowing that even your happiness is something which they can't share with you, realising that perhaps you won't return to them from this other world denied to them, or if you return you may come back quite changed. Last night in the tube there was a young girl with a sweet and sensitive face and she was very drunk: there was nothing one could do for her but she seemed so defenceless and so utterly oblivious and one hoped that no harm would come to her. Love is the same sort of intoxication, don't you think? But I was glad you were in love and I was grateful to Stella for making you happy. I am trying very hard to have faith; perhaps women find it naturally more difficult than men because instinctively they interfere more, and feel personally involved, in the lives of those near to them. Unless I can cultivate faith I shall worry if Gaga M. flies in an aeroplane or Mole goes out alone in a boat, and make both their lives hell, as well as my own. One must trust that life is planned regardless of our own efforts to distort the flow of it. Believing this has made it easier when you have been in danger and I suppose it explains how these amazing women exist even when their sons and brothers and husbands are constantly in fearful danger.

Then your next letter came with a photograph of Stella and she looked so sweet and unfrightening I felt ashamed that I should ever have doubted that you could have been hurt except by losing her. I do hope you didn't hate leaving her too much. I suppose knowing that it had to come made it easier.

There is a girl we met recently who is now married to a friend of Leslie's. She is 26 and very fascinating with a lovely sense of humour, intelligent, sensitive and very unlike all the masses of ordinary attractive people one sees and finds so uninspiring. She looks a little like your photograph of Stella. I am telling you this because she has a young sister (unmarried) and I am hoping to meet her and if she is half as charming I will keep a special eye on her for you.

145

Sicily must be lovely after Egypt but to see it in the midst of a war must seem so wrong. The background for war seems to be desert or muddy trenches but not all the unsophisticated charm of orchards and countryside. I am very thankful you were not among the first assaults and I hope any future entries you may have to make to other countries will be suitably delayed, but I hate to think of you even so near the fighting. I wonder if Italy will give in and what of Germany now? What do you think of it all? Do you hear anything more than the news we get?

It is quite grotesque for you to say your letters are boring. They seem to combine every virtue of really witty letter writing and I am not alone and prejudiced about this as I read bits to lots of people who obviously find them as amusing and entertaining as I do.

I agree with you entirely about Graham Greene's books. I believe he is usually in a state of acute alcoholism which may taint his general view of life if he writes during the aftermath and is suffering from a furry tongue and jaundiced eye. I think personal hatred must be more passionate than the indirect kind. I can get much hotter about a few cads in England than atrocities in Poland, which is probably all wrong but less far removed.

Your Stella has a lovely figure. It is incredible anyone can look so attractive in service uniform! She looks so young for so many accomplishments – I had imagined a rather Oppenheim charmer!

I love your personal ad from the man seeking work in a convent. One visualises the most delicious possibilities.

Have you been able often to employ your famous word *fabuletto*? Those days in Italy seem so remote and yet quite recent in spite of it being such years ago. One feels that war years should not count in a lifetime but should be quietly ignored. There are three letters I have on one side which I think I have already answered. Two are letter-cards J & K and

146

then there is one long letter J dated June 17th. You had just been to see *You Were Never Lovelier* and it had made you think of the old days at Nic. & Wat.[1] Your description of it all made my tummy turn over with nostalgia. I suppose we did know that war was imminent and the world in a landslide to destruction but there were so many ways of forgetting it. I suppose we feel about it all as the last generation felt about the Gay Nineties and, like their era, I doubt if ours will ever return. I can see years of food rationing and utility clothes and I cringe at the thought of it but no matter how bleak the future may be from the point of view of luxurious living we have got our memories. I have been reading *A Time for Greatness* by Herbert Agar and he predicts a levelling up and down on the lines of Sweden. I couldn't bear London with none of the fantastic and glamorous side, as it is now and that's another reason I would prefer a new life in the country where there are no comparisons to be made. It is easier to stand fear and terror and uncertainty than plain, squalid boredom and grey hum-drum living but I suppose we had such constant stimulus of excitement before the war that it has spoiled us for quiet and uneventful living. I am entirely in sympathy with your early-bedding. Before Mole's arrival we couldn't get there fast enough and spent every free afternoon having snoozes. The Mole has changed all that but it is only force of circumstance and will soon return!

Pops has just telephoned. The six-minute maximum which is now allowed is hopelessly inadequate to say anything. I often giggle about our chats with Mops which invariably began, 'Now say what you want to say and be quick as I am listening to a very good wireless programme.' It used to make you laugh so much you were quite incapable of saying anything.

We went to see *Mission to Moscow* the other evening. It is

---

[1] The family-owned publisher, Nicholson & Watson

extremely well done and well worth seeing even though it stresses our hopeless policy before the war. We also saw Colonel Blimp but I was so fixed with Low's ideas that I couldn't accustom myself to the theory that he is a fine old gentleman and the backbone of the country.

Mole is growing rapidly. He stands on his feet and hands and peers back between his very wobbling fat knees and then topples down flat on his face which exasperates him a lot. He adores his feedies and for lunch knocks back some broth, a plate of vegetables and some sort of pudding. He finds the broth rather boring as his passion is a good dollop of spinach or carrots which he eats, smacking his lips at each mouthful and tasting it like a connoisseur. He is very brown and has an adorable sunsuit which is almost a Hartnell model and consists of very brief trousers, a large pocket and an Eton collar. His hair is making rapid progress and he has now three hairs which we brush into a tuft on the top and the rest is almost unobservable. Each morning I give him a cold spray – he opens his eyes very wide and blows out his cheeks and is very pleased when it is over! For tea he has a sandwich which he drops constantly on the carpet. He picks it up by scratching feverishly at it with his podgy index finger and then shutting his hand tightly over it. It is very baffling for him to know what to do with it next to get it into his mouth so he ends by trying to suck out the rather squashed mess between his two fingers. I'm sure ice-cream will be his Utopia!

I feel I could go on writing to you for ages but the Mole will be waking soon for his final smackerel and I don't suppose I shall have another chance to write for some days, so I will finish this off and try to write again very soon. It is such a comfort to feel I can talk to you each night and be close to you even if life is too difficult to allow much time for writing. At times, if I am depressed and life seems too bloody, I think of you and the thought of your love and all that it means to me keeps me sane and makes me feel that I am greatly blessed and with patience the war will end and you will be home again. Until then, you will continue to be for ever in my thoughts and always in my prayers.

D

‿᷍‿

Lieut G.A. Watson
522 Coy R.A.S.C. 50 (N) Div
C.M.F.[1]

August 13th, 1943

Beloved,

The Moles are doing well by their outcast. One post brought me a very long letter from you (60), a letter-card (62), and I have already acknowledged 61, – and a large bag from Papa Mole including a very amusing long letter, a letter-card and a postcard of such hideous hues that Scotland itself must have been combed to produce it. Actually, coming from Kilmelford brought back inevitably memories of better days. I went there from Cambridge with John and Terence.[2] I only remember scanty details of the visit – my first to Scotland in my capacity as a fisherman. We fished one day in Scammerdale – a long, low, rather beautiful loch – perhaps you went there. I was the only one to catch a fish which so annoyed Terence and John, who were teaching me to fish, that they threw it back saying it was too small to keep. This, I know, sounds too good to be true, but I swear by it. Terence, too, regaled me with stories of the art of loving. The only thing I remember him saying in this

---

[1] Central Mediterranean Forces
[2] Terence Horsley, then editor of the *Sunday Times*

connection was that no kiss was worth having unless you got your face slapped – a *bon mot* that I have since quoted to good effect in the Mess. On such small threads hang the reputations of your local Don Juan. As I am the local butt of our Mess you can imagine what I have had to endure since liaising with Miss Divinska: I am the accredited correspondent of the Yugo-Slav Free Press; I have already accepted the job as Ambassador at Belgrade after the war; I spend most of my time cruising up the Dalmatian coast supplying General Mihailovitch by submarine. 522 Coy has become Yugo-Slavic conscious. (I do not suffer in silence – although, perhaps, suffer is hardly the appropriate word.) I have, of course, been sent to Sicily because Alex was too hot to hold me. Thus do the cruel and licentious soldiery amuse themselves.

Life continues to be relatively slothful. As at the moment I imagine English fruit is relatively plentiful I feel I can speak of our own fruit situation without making your mouth water. Having spent so long on a cultivation-less desert it is still my principal interest in life. Since last writing you we have moved from an almond orchard to a lemon grove. When one gets thirsty one reaches up, plucks half a dozen big fat lemons and makes lemon squash. Across the road is a field hanging with muscatel grapes, melons, tomatoes, cucumbers, almonds, corn-on-the-cob all there for the picking. I dearly wish I could send you some home – and if you could send me a Cox's Orange Pippin that would be nice, too.

I can so easily understand your longing for the war to finish. A home to make, a son to bring up, a husband to look after – so natural to long for the peace and quiet in which to do such rational and normal things. I suppose after four years of war it is natural that one should become like a dopey animal with all one's sense and sensibility blunted. The future to which one looks forward is still so impossibly remote. The present with its frustration, loneliness, and boredom and unhappiness is still so horribly at hand. I can't offer you any bromides except, perhaps, that ninety-nine per cent of humanity are feeling to a greater or lesser degree the same. We sold ourselves to the devil and now we are paying the bill and he will exact the last farthing of damages. However, things aren't all black. Three years after the war started we were living on hope that we should win it. Now, twelve months later, a miracle has happened and we know we shall win with a confidence based on solid foundations. The war may go on another two years. It may easily end by Xmas. Nobody outside the know can estimate the factors that will bring a sudden collapse. Our bombing, our blockade, the fall of Italy, the advance of Russia, an invasion, any of these factors taken together or separately might cause the Germans to say we have lost – and once they believe they have lost, they collapse suddenly: *vide* Tunisia. Neither you nor I can tell how strongly these factors are operating but it would be idiotic to ignore them and merely view the war as a territorial advance with the end coming when our troops are fighting in the suburbs of Berlin. So hope on, D, and do not put too much store by the passing days. If the war ends in two years' time you will have lost six years: you will still have another forty to look forward to. And in some ways you will be better for the six. As to ages, there is a tendency to think that one time in life is better than another. I wonder. Does the man of fifty not enjoy himself as much as the man of twenty-five. It is natural, but a false statement, to look on anything in the past as best but in fact it is because past pain cannot be remembered, only past pleasures. And new wine is horribly rank and immature. I have probably bored you with all this, but I am as weary of the war as you are and I honestly believe it to be true.

Will you tell me how long this letter takes to reach you? There are no more air-mail letters so this will have to come by surface. If it takes a long time I shall have to write letter-cards in future but, as you say, they are horribly confining.

I loved your photos of Whitton. In two there are bits cut out of you with no explanation offered. I can only assume you had spilt some marmalade down your collar at breakfast. Tell G. Mole I am very surprised to see he wears uniform on leave. If the reason is that you have had all his suits made into costumes for yourself I have an old fishing jersey and some white flannels which are a bit short in the leg which he is welcome to. Mole, of course, looks – and sounds – enchanting. I am sorry to think I shall never see him retreating, in some indignation, from his objective.

You are not the only one who hears from Pops in a moralising way. Bless him, he doesn't do it much but when he has a chance offered him he finds it hard to resist. He seemed to consider that my sitting in a truck with a pick-halve ready to brain an Egyptian was definitely due to the brutalising influence of war. 'After all, you might have been born an Egyptian yourself. You must try and understand them in their ignorance'!!! When I mentioned Stella to fill up space in one of my letters I made the reference as vague as possible. He can't make up his mind about two alternatives: a) I am going to marry her; b) I am going to contract syphilis. Quite certainly he thinks she is a harpy. 'You must remember that a life of loneliness is apt to cloud one's judgment in matters of human-relationships.' However, I mustn't be unkind because he is really only thinking of me. But I can't help smiling. I feel that I am in a better position to decide the merits of Stella and Egyptians than he is. And, after all, D, I wasn't born an Egyptian. I wasn't really.

Dinner is up and the Mess is getting talkative so I must stop this now. Pray God it won't be long before we are together again.

Your very loving brother,

G

⤙⤚

September 27th, 1943

D, darling,

I received your lovely long letter (64) of August 8th a couple of days ago and I have been meaning to answer it ever since. It was sweet of you – but I expected it – to be so understanding about Stella. Actually, it seems such ages ago and so much has happened since that it's merely a very sweet memory in the rather misty vales of the past. It was, of course, obviously – because of the nature of things – only an interlude and could have no permanence attached to it.

As you will have heard I am now in Italy – and very pleasant it is. The scenery is gorgeous. We climb up two or three thousand feet on hair-raising winding roads with loaded three tonners and then as suddenly drop down sheer over the other side. It makes our routine supply runs fun. The people are shockingly poor and half-starved and most of the towns have been pretty hardly dealt with by the R.A.F. The people are only now beginning to stream back from the hills. Their constant cry is '*biscotti*'. I am picking up a smattering of Italian – about equal to my knowledge of Arabic, although I haven't discovered the equivalent of 'bugger off' yet (I can say that in three ways in Arabic!).

Just recently, I've been organising and producing a company concert which was held last night and was a triumphant success. We had a lot of vino laid on – we were taking no chances! I wrote a couple of numbers and compèred the whole outfit, introducing each turn. I'm told that I shook them considerably and, between you and me, I think I was pretty funny though I'm glad Pops wasn't there to hear most of my jokes. We've got quite a lot of very good talent. It's one of the things on the credit side of the army so far as I'm concerned, that it's cured me of any self-consciousness I ever had in appearing in public. I would, without any sense of embarrassment, recite the sixty verses – if I knew them – of Eskimo Nell, standing on my head – if I could – naked before the King – if he ever asked me to. However, I'm afraid that public entertaining will in peace time be of rather a different proposition to in war, where one can make topical allusions to a very receptive audience.

The other day I went bathing and swam across a bay. When I got to the other side, I found I hadn't the strength to swim back, so I had to walk back to my clothes through the village street, stark naked. The men were delighted and so – I think – were the Italian women sitting in the street. What a life!

Lovingly,

G

꿍

Very darling G,

I sent you a longish letter only about 10 days ago and since then not a morsel of news has occurred, not even a smell of gossip, which is very paradoxical. Usually, I have too much to say and no time to write it and now I have a most delectable quantity of time and nothing to say of any interest. Having received this warning you would be wiser to read no further!

We are at Crinan and three days of our leave have passed – three sodden days of rain which have more than proved my suspicion that my mackintosh is laughably un-waterproof. The gulls swerve and swoop against a grey blanket of sky and the islands are blotted out by a curtain of solidly falling rain. Yet it is heavenly to be here, and there is pleasure even in the sound of the gulls and the noise of the rain and to smell the wood in the burning log fire and to know that no shattering call of a Mole will destroy the idle moment.

We were talking of the Mole and discussing the main essentials of his up-bringing. It is not an easy problem and there seem to be two alternatives. Either one can attempt to train him to the conventional world most adapted to fit into our far from satisfactory society of today, or one regards the demands of society as unimportant and obstructive and tries instead to make him think and behave as an individual. Either you teach him to play the 'right' games, to be accomplished in the 'right' sports, to have a superficial smattering of the fashionable cultural interests or you leave him to develop himself, let him have leisure to stretch his mind, his limbs and his instincts as he pleases: make known to him all the fascinating alternatives the world has to offer but not insist that his education should include the ability to play golf, bridge and all the other social exchanges.

What would you do? Do tell me as it seems to me the two approaches to life are so fundamentally different that it isn't possible to compromise and surely if one's ambition is to attain a standard of social proficiency one automatically turns into a standard product which makes life easier possibly, but much more limited. When I was younger, I longed to do the right things and suffered considerably because I had not been brought up along those lines. It seemed embarrassing that, unlike other girls, I never suffered the precipitate projection into society known as Coming Out; I felt at a loss when conversation was not an exchange of ideas but a competition of how many names one could claim acquaintance with, which could be found lurking on the dimmer pages of *Who's Who*. Even my tennis was a source of shame – my ambition to get the ball over the net with as much vigour as possible was clearly out of place, as only the manner in which one placed the ball there seemed to be of importance. I don't want the Mole to reproach me as I secretly reproached Mops for not seeing that I was not adequately provided with these accomplishments. Yet are they important? Have they any intrinsic value? Don't these very accomplishments make it difficult to see life except through second rate eyes, to think secondhand thoughts and to feel second best re-actions? I am convinced that a child should be fitted for the world and not only to become a social marionette but if you start a child off with a sense of inferiority, and lack of confidence because he has not mastered the social graces will he not attach too much importance to them? I don't know, do you?

I have been thinking a lot about life after the war, as has everybody else, no doubt. This question of Public Schools being replaced by State education; the possibility that domestic service will be regarded as a medieval and unholy practice. It is so difficult to be impartial and disinterested. All my instincts clamour for life to remain as it was: I like to be waited on, I like to be one of a privileged class, I like to feel a divine right of completely unearned being. Yet obviously the whole things is so grossly unfair; obviously these things can't be provided for except at the expense of somebody else. Mrs Froggatt[1] is exactly my age; she is a person of extreme honesty, sensibility and character and a very much finer person than a great many of my leisured friends. For her, life has been one long struggle and anxiety and soul-destroying work which makes a horrid comparison by the side of my own pleasant existence. Yet surely for us all to take in our own washing is not a very sensible or economic proceeding?

---

[1] Leslie's batman's wife

Either life will be intolerably uncomfortable for everyone, or drones will still be able to continue their luxurious existence undisturbed. I suppose the original injustice is inherited money but not many men will accumulate fortunes if the government take the whole of it on death and, even so, it is hard on the children accustomed to living with their millionaire father to then have to accustom themselves to the pauper level.

There are some very amusing people staying in the hotel. Not spectacular but with the ability to talk intelligently and be amusing in a grim Scottish way. I think the average Scottish pub produces this type more than the English and unlike an English hotel lounge there are long periods of time when the Scottish nose is fixed firmly into his book and not a word is uttered. I am struck by the quantity of unmarried women one meets in Scotland, or perhaps it is just they are more enterprising than the English spinster who prefers to cling to her virgin hearth rather than wander abroad.

One of the men here is an old Reptonian called Morton but he was there before you, though had a brother there later on. Oddly enough, he knows Terence and was going to collaborate with him on some film release which never came off. Another odd thing happened when old Captain Cameron of the *Otranto,* on which we sailed to Australia, suddenly appeared for lunch. He is in charge of the life-boats and spends his time sailing them to their different stations after they have been overhauled. He simply loves the work, but it was odd to see him standing at the wheel of a 13½ ton vessel after the 20,000 ton *Otranto*! The lock keeper had a very poor opinion of his seamanship and complained that he handled every vessel like a liner. If it had been fine he would have let us sail with him to Oban which would have been heavenly. We went on board while they went through the locks and there is something very thrilling about a tough little sailing boat. It made me think of our beautiful launch which we took up the Thames. Watching some of the many taking their motor launches through the locks convinces me that our handling was relatively expert!

It's odd how emotion clouds one's sense of judgment and humour. I was thinking about that first night when Germany had declared war on Poland. More than the sensation of terror which, I remember at the time was most acute, I remember my pleasure at being referred to as 'the little man'. Now I ask you in cold blood could anything be more utterly nauseating? I am too much of a feminist to relish my sex being mistaken or unappreciated and the term 'little man' in itself is always used about some inferior being like a non-conformist minister or someone of whom one feels equally patronising. (I remember a humourous article of P. Fleming on the subject.) If one's sex must be ignored surely the added ignominy of being little is too much? But no! I was pleased. It seemed splendidly in keeping with all fake sentiment of Keep the Home Fires Burning and Pack Up Your Troubles. There I was a billowing feminine figure in my badly cut trousers facing most bravely and intrepidly sudden death and I don't know what with a proud light in my eye because I was 'the little man'. I shall keep that one from my grandchildren. When they cling to my knee begging for details of how Granny faced the war, I shall be Florence Nightingale or Nurse Cavell but not 'little man'.

I must bring this extremely boring letter to 'a close'. You must admit that considering nothing of any value or interest has been said that vast spaces of expensive blue notepaper have been covered.

Gaga Mole is threatening to write to you but at present he is too deeply engrossed in your copy of Douglas Reed's *All Our Tomorrows*. He is bitterly complaining that my letters to you cost him a fortune in cigarettes.

We are both wondering if you will be with us on our next

visit here. Kilmelford is incomparably less alluring. The last time I was here the Mole had just begun to make his presence known and coming back again with a detached Mole in 'Other parts' makes his existence seem almost unreal. I seemed then to be starting off on some endless and rather alarming journey from which I would never return and yet here I am feeling as ordinary as before. It is kind of Time to creep so silently by that one is left unaware of the breath of her passing. If there were no mirrors we should not have the slightest suspicion that our hair had turned grey and our faces wrinkled, so gently does youth slip away from us. When one is very young you imagine the operation to be sharp, painful and deliberate. So perhaps we slide from the consciousness of life to the unawareness of death.

The Major[2] has just finished a book of Pops' choosing called *Puritan's Progress* in which the author describes the effects of a fiercely non-conformist upbringing. He believes that it was the cause of robbing him of all confidence in himself. I wondered if that was why we, as a family, seem to suffer a completely unwarranted inferiority complex?

Bless you, darling brother. I never cease to think of you. The joy of your letters makes your absence tolerable and the unbreakable bond of understanding which is between us comforts my loneliness for you.

D

❧

In November, the 8th Army returned to England to prepare itself for the invasion of France. During this period, the correspondence between Diana and Graham ceased.

❧

---

[2] Leslie had been recently promoted

Rothbury

Wednesday, April 19th, 1944

Darling G,

Life seems so uncertain that I am sending you the enclosed
letter for you to keep unopened until, and if, the second front
begins and you are sent abroad. I hope it will remain unread
but I like to feel that, however futile it is, you shall have it to
take with you if you leave England suddenly.

I had a very nice reply to my letter from Charles Morgan
today and I will send it on to you after Hazel has seen it. I am
going to York to see her, with the parents, for the night on
Friday. He says, 'I hope your brother has good fortune. Send
him my wishes.' He was a naval officer before becoming an
author and is now in the Admiralty with a son at Eton who is
about to join the Grenadier Guards. He writes in the *Times Lit
Supp* but has no new novel in view.

I wish you had been with us last weekend. We went for a
lovely walk with Mops leading far in advance. Pops, wearing
his foreign office hat and black overcoat, paused by the
wayside to prod out each dandelion, while I was the
intermediate link feeling rather in need of a motor bike to
keep my convoy together!

Ring up some time if you get the chance. I would love to talk
to you again. I am staying here until the 29th unless London
becomes unpleasant in which case I will stay on with Simon
indefinitely.

Forgive this scrawl but I am writing in bed and it is time for a
bit of O.B.D.[1]

Good-night my dearest one and blessings.

Ever, D

✃✃

---

[1] On the backs down

Rothbury,

April 19th, 1944

My very beloved brother,

I can't bear to think that you are gone again. The dread of
this moment has been like a cold fog in my heart ever since
you came home. It is so difficult to go on holding fast; like
our walk back from Dunoon at Crinan when it grew dusk and
the rain beat in our faces and the way seemed endless, but we
knew that we would get home if we plodded solidly on with
our heads against the wind, and, comforted, because we were
doing it together. So the end will come to this hellish war and
you will be home again.

It is such anguish to know that you are going back into
danger and I pray that the faith and prayers of all of us who
love you may, with God's will, protect and shield you always.

The pride I have in you, and the love I feel for you, twist my
heart with an ache and longing and I hate to feel that my
share of the burden is so unequal to yours. All I can do is to
try to be worthy of the things you have shown me and keep a
steadfast faith and courage to face the future.

I am writing this at Whitton where every familiar thing
speaks to me of you. You seem so near that at any moment
the door might open and I should feel no surprise to see you
standing there. I am glad that Norfolk Road[1] is full of your
loved presence and that you know my 'shipyard tornado'.
Perhaps before next spring you will be back again and we
shall know it is for always. This time the end is in sight and we
know that we shall win. This time I feel more certain of God's
loving care and less frightened to trust. I wonder if it is easier
for you than before?

---

[1] Diana and Leslie's London house

161

Outside the wind is blowing a gale and the rain is beating against the windows. I am sitting alone over the fire where we have often sat and talked together, after the others had gone to bed. Now it seems unreal as though I had slipped back into a past that is always there, at one with the present and the future.

Oh, my darling G, there is nothing I can say which you don't already know more deeply than any words can say. You know that life without you is not life at all, that your love is one of life's greatest treasures and that my pride in you and love for you are a fire that can never be quenched. We have some very precious memories which stretch back from when we were very young to the Repton and Cambridge days[2], Bruton Place, Carrington House, Eaton Square and finally Norfolk Road. Beguiling cross-words, train journeys north, Whitton and now Crinan are all words which mean so much.

Good-night, my very precious brother, may God be with you and keep you and bring you safely home. I will talk to you each night until we meet again.

With all my prayers, my thoughts and blessings,

D

❧❧

---

[2] My public school and university

Lieut G.A. Watson
522 Coy R.A.S.C. (Inf. Bde.)
A.P.O.[1] – Eng.

April 22nd, 1944

My darlingest D,

I am orderly dog and the Mess is empty so it is a good opportunity to write to you and answer your letter. Actually, it is not so good an opportunity as appears on the surface. A cinema tent is functioning about fifty yards away and the tent here is filled with the roar of the sound-track. I don't think anything sounds more ridiculous than a sound-track of a film unseen. It has the wireless licked to a standing-start. Such is one of the benefits of modern civilization. Perhaps the future will know it as sizzleization, he cracked merrily.

I went to the same cinema last night to see *Claudia* which was a nifty piece of voluptuousness. Pops would have had a fit.

It was lovely getting your letter. The enclosure I shall cherish dearly, unread, until I need it. I guess I will. There's a lot I'd like to say about this invasion but I don't know how to put it into words. First of all you mustn't think that I feel about it like you do, like I would have done if I'd gone into it straight from civilian life. You see the army, deliberately or not, blunts one's sensibilities and builds up a very hard core of protective tissue round them. Thus one gradually gets so hardened to any demand that is made on one that one accepts it unquestioningly without considering too much the implications. Thus one takes on undertakings in a routine fashion that would cause a civilian to flap around for days at the prospect. For your own peace of mind you must believe

---

[1] Army Post Office

this. When this invasion starts I shall naturally hate it. But I can't somehow worry about it till it does start. I was far more upset this week at the prospect of going to the dentist. Now, during the actual invasion there are about four things which can happen. (a) I can get through unscathed. I reckon the chances of this are 10–1 on during the first week, 25–1 for the first month, 50–1 there after. If I'm ok, there's no need to worry. (b) I can be taken prisoner. I reckon the chances are 50–1 against. Anyhow, if I do why worry? I'm out of the war. (c) I can be wounded. Chances? 10–1 against. But if I get wounded the chances are 1000–13 (see official figures) I don't die. So why worry? I do a bit, actually, I don't mind a clean wound, but I should hate one in the guts. Chances 1000–15 against (see official figures). Long odds when you consider the figures of those wounded and not. Still, I agree, a nasty thought. (d) I might get killed. Well, if I do, it will upset you, Hazel, Mops and Pops, Leslie. It won't upset me because I shan't know about it. As to after life, I don't know. But I do know that death will only be a very temporary separation from those one loves. So the only thing against death is the unhappiness it will cause you five. And if you are wise you won't be unhappy because you'll know (a) it is only a temporary parting. (b) I shall, in a sense, and a very real sense, be as much beside you as ever. That I know you believe anyhow. So you see, reduced to its bare bones it's silly to worry about this invasion even if one didn't believe, as you do, and I do, that I would get through safely. But, actually I do worry a little – not very much, but a little. I worry because I am scared of being frightened, of doing something cowardly. Now I know, of course, that I shall be frightened, who isn't under fire, but I pray every night that I won't show it. And when I'm most frightened I shall think of you – particularly during an air-raid – and your courage and try and get courage from it. The thing that scares me is that one has no mental control over fear – or only very little – when one's frightened the body does things you don't want it to do. So, D. darling, if you want to pray for me, don't pray for my safety but pray that I shall be given courage whatever may happen to me. Actually, everybody in the know is wildly optimistic about the whole affair and don't think it will be half as difficult as it's made out.

It's horrid to be going away again but it's been a lovely five months. Think, I've seen you three times on leave and once for a week in London. I shall go abroad again refreshed and heartened, sure in the knowledge we are nearing the end, fortified with your happiness in Leslie and Simon and helped by some further lovely memories. Do you remember meeting me on the steps of your house in overalls – a minute dreamed of for three years. And we were a bit embarrassed and didn't quite know what to say. Do you remember me finishing the dregs of your champagne to your intense annoyance and Pops reading the labels on the bottle? Do you remember having tea at the Percy Arms, beer in the pub in Alnwick after that lovely run over the moors, beer at Whittingham when Mops felt naughty going into the public bar. (Rather a boozy memory.) Do you remember flapping round the train like an elderly goose on your way to Crinan – but why pretend that one moment of that glorious weekend in a glorious place was any better than any others. O beloved D, when one can have memories as rich as that in war-time what have we to fear of the future? We are, indeed, blessed. I shall say nothing – because I need say nothing of what your love has meant to me and what fun has come out of it. Meantime, we are within sight of the end and I believe that God in his kindness will save us to enjoy it.

But whatever should happen to me I make it a trust that you will not allow the event to cast its shadow over the future. If it did, all our past happiness would have been at too great a cost. The parting, if any, like this one will be but temporary.

165

Incidentally, I shall continue to talk to you each night in bed. My pride in you, and my love of you, and my happiness because of you, is immense. God bless you.

G

P.S. Please stay at Whitton if the raids get bad.

❧

Extract from a letter to my parents from the Normandy Bridgehead, dated June 13th, 1944:

I sent you a field post-card a few days back to let you know I was ok. I have not had time to write before. In fact, I have been busier than I have ever been before, working (hard) an average of a twenty-hour day since I landed. However, things are a bit easier at the moment, so I will at any rate make a start of a letter.

What can I say about the invasion that has not already been said by better pens than mine? For travelling, the company was split over several ships. For myself, I had with me a few lorries and men and these we embarked four or five days before we sailed. The great day of sailing arrived with a minimum of excitement and emotion – having been post-poned for 24 hours because of the weather. Any post-ponement by that time was unwelcome – we wanted to get the inevitable over – and we wished ardently for fine weather. In fact, the next day was worse and in the evening of June 5, we slid silently out onto the rough waters of the Channel and had our last view of England from the heavily laden deck of an American Tank Landing Ship that was rolling like hell. These boats are built to beach, are flat bottomed, and what they do in a rough sea is nobody's business. Very soon a large proportion were sick – and remained so. I went to bed and awoke next morning to see the coast of France – it was as easy as that – and a vast, breath-taking, awe-inspiring collection of ships of every size packed like herrings. By that time, the assault forces had been ashore five hours and everything was as calm and peaceful as a Cowes regatta. It was incredible. I was due to land six hours after the assault – in fact I landed twenty-four hours after. For those twenty-four hours we lay off the shore trying to get in but it was too rough. We began to wonder whether they could get the stuff on shore quick enough but next day it got calmer and a breath-taking flood of guns, lorries, tanks etc. poured up the beach. In fact, we had as peaceful a twenty-four hours as could be imagined except for a little – very little – bombing at night. Why the Germans let a target like that go untouched is one of those unsolved mysteries of the war.

However, on the evening of June 7th I was ashore, in contact with my company and issuing ammunition to a gun-thirsty Division. Since then, I've done nothing else – collect and issue – collect and issue all day, practically all night. It's been grand fun on the whole and I've never felt I've done a more needed job so well since I've been in the army.

Next morning

Having said things were quieting down we got a rush job through which kept me up all night. It's amazing really how little sleep one can get along with when one has to. Everybody ashore is in terrific spirits, working like hell and really feeling that this time the worst is over and we are on the final stretch.

Looking back on the invasion it was a very welcome anti-climax. One foresaw, and grew accustomed to, the idea of every type of unpleasantness. In fact, it was absurdly easy. I speak for myself. I don't suppose the assault troops found it much fun. As for the emotional excitement there was nil. I

167

suppose one approached the whole thing in such gradual stages one came on the ultimate without being aware of it. First the freedom of Bournemouth, then a camp, then confined to camp, then embarking, then standing by ready to sail. At the end of it all, one sailed with no feeling at all. In that way, the army is very good in its tactics.

I must stop this. More customers have loomed up.

৵৶

Capt. G.A. Watson
522 Coy R.A.S.C. (Inf. Bde.),
A.P.O. England.

June 20th, 1944

Very beloved D,

At time of writing I am sitting under an apple tree in the orchard of a big farm house.[1] I rather go for fruit trees – in Sicily it was olives and almonds, here it is apples but, alas, pas de pommes. (I speak de lingo veera goot, no?) Which reminds me of the true story of a man in this unit when he came to France in 1940. He couldn't tell his wife where he was so he wrote, 'This is a most amazing country – even the little children can speak French fluently.' But to return to the background sketching. The sun is shining out of a very watery sky. Yesterday was a perfect stinken boche and it never stopped raining. I got wettish and my wog wig-wam made out of odd pieces of tarpaulin and in which I have my residence began to look a bit sorry for itself. At its best it looks like something spewed up by a pre-fabricated house. Of course in Egypt weather was no problem and all one asked of a shelter was shade. In Europe one has to guard against things that go

---

[1] A mile or so from Arromanches

168

drip in the night. Around me, stretched in profusion and confusion are my wares, i.e. stacks of ammunition. I can hear you say, 'but how dangerous.' This is a common fallacy. Ammunition, with minor exceptions in the explosive line, is not dangerous until fired – then it tends to be.

What is there to say about the Invasion?

Living I live, as stated in a wog wig-wam, in an orchard.

Food We eat tinned food eked out by what we can buy locally which is very little. E.g. Breakfast: sausages and bacon and biscuits. Lunch: some form of scraggy meat, mixed compote of vegetables, very good steamed puddings, treacle, marmalade, ginger, rice. Tea: biscuits and cheese. Supper. See lunch, only lighter. In addition, we get a bar of chocolate, seven cigarettes and some boiled sweets each day. Local purchase provides occasional fresh vegetables – potatoes, cabbage, onions, Camembert cheese – very good – a little bread – strictly rationed and buying illegal – an occasional egg and cider. Wine is wickedly expensive, e.g. 15/- for vin blanc and very scarce. In addition, we brought over a N.A.A.F.I. pack which includes one bar of soap, one razor blade, fifty cigarettes each a week. In addition, we brought over and have now drunk a little whisky.

Laundry My batman washes all my things.

Work I supply the Division with ammunition. That is to say, I hold a stock of their requirements. They come back to draw from me and I send back still further to replenish my stocks. We are kept busy – very busy – just now, but it's good fun. I have to help me a staff sergeant, two sergeants, a corporal and some loaders. Things are getting slacker now but for the first ten days we averaged four hours sleep a night. Some nights we didn't get any.

Enemy action Touch wood – none. At night sporadic and widely dispersed bombing – nothing at all to worry about. By day the R.A.F. reigns almost completely supreme.

Washing We have all had one bath already in some baths in a nearby town. For the rest, a camp wash-stand and some hot water.

Civilians Some very friendly – hysterically so. Some overtly hostile. Most surly and uninterested. I have met very few so I can't speak generally. Naturally, one doesn't wax enthusiastically about having one's country fought over.

Our troops Amazing morale. Working and fighting till they drop and asking for more. Looking on life with the attitude 'we've waited for this and now they'll get it.' I don't suppose they've ever felt so savage or more determined to let nothing or nobody stand in their way. If de Gaulle tries any hanky-panky God help him.[2]

Of the Invasion itself I have already written in a letter to the parents. There was nothing to be frightened at and the whole thing was quite amazing. Of course it was all over by the time I got there and I cannot emphasise enough the difference in the hardships borne by the fighting troops and us rear-line wallahs. Still, even their casualties were lighter than expected. In this Coy we didn't lose a man.

Your very devoted,

G

※

---

[2] General de Gaulle had a notoriously bad relationship with Churchill

Capt. G.A. Watson
522 Coy R.A.S.C. (Inf. Bde.)
B.E.F.[1]

July 3rd, 1944

Darlingest D,

I look out on a lovely evening after days of monotonous rain. We certainly have not been lucky in our weather or are European summers always like this? It is so long since I experienced one, I forget! Actually, for the R.A.S.C., rain is nothing more than an inconvenience. It is disagreeable to have one's dump made into a squelching morasse; it is irritating to feel one's beret (did you know I wore a beret now?) shrinks every time one puts it on afresh; it becomes tedious having wet mackintoshes dripping water over one's papers in the office. But it is no more than an inconvenience. For the infantry lying out in their holes, wet to the skin, it must be purgatory. I hope that tonight's sun is presage of finer weather – and not – as so often of late – a temporary flash-in-the-pan.

Tonight I had my first strawberries. I have been eyeing them ripen in the garden for some days but owing to the new-found generosity of the farmer who keeps giving me things, I have not liked to ask for any. However, tonight I saw his wife working in the garden and in exchange for some cigarettes got a couple of handfuls. Local purchase has not – to date – been a success, largely because of the enormous number of troops in a small area. Now there is an order out prohibiting all buying of food. It will be impossible to enforce it but I can see the sense of it. It is silly to let troops buy food that will later be needed for starving Europe. On

---

[1] British Expeditionary Force

the other hand, the army should make arrangements to buy and issue perishable goods that would otherwise be wasted. Actually, we are adequately fed, but speaking for myself I find it practically impossible eating the tinned meat-cum-stew that has replaced the almost as unpalatable bully-beef.

Life here is becoming rurally obstetric. In this orchard there is an enormous bull who looks a little like Dudley. He is chained to a minute peg in the ground which he could uproot with one good pull. So far, this idea has not entered his head, though I live in daily expectation of it. Yesterday, they brought in a cow to be what is politely known as served, I believe. It was incredibly unsatisfying for all concerned, the whole performance taking about fifteen seconds. I was a bit worried, so I asked the farm, '*Succés?*' '*Magnifique, monsieur, trés magnifique.*' Today, they led in a day-old calf – but I can't believe it was as quick as that. Then we had two jack donkeys fighting. Apparently they always do if they get together. One had escaped from a nearby farm and they kicked each other and brayed at each other in the height of mutual fury. The French don't believe in castrating their animals for some reason.

Next evening

At that point I was interrupted – first by Boule Baker,[2] who came in and told me that he had always wanted to live a life nearer to nature and the army gave him the opportunity. I asked him whether he intended to stay on in it but he said he didn't! Then Krantz[3] arrived and said that if he had to look any longer at a certain red face, piggy eyes and bull neck he would have to vomit. We drank a glass of cider to his damnation but it does not seem to have had any success. He

---

[2] Regimental colleague with a nickname which had become Frenchified
[3] Linden, hence Lindenkrantz, hence Krantz

is quite as revolting today, but unquestionably damned. Then the red face, piggy eyes and bull necked appeared in person and told me the General was going to inspect my dump this morning. I'd heard that before so took no precautions other than putting on a clean shirt. The General did not inspect the dump, so I am annoyed about the shirt but alas the damage has been done.

Today's obstetric news consists in the arrival of twelve newly-born ducklings. They have already strayed into my batman's shelter and with a uniformity that would do credit to a Tiller girl[4] apparently all spent a penny. One of the men received a letter from his wife hoping that he was enjoying camping out in such nice weather. In the ensuing discussion I discovered from amidst the blasphemy that it was the general consensus of opinion that after the war the following were on the banned list: picnics, stews, bully-beef, the seaside – if sandy – queues and CAMPING OUT! CAMPING OUT!! CAMPING OUT!!!

This letter is like the jet plane and progresses by fits and starts. I have just been away for an hour with Krantz. He said that if he had to sit another minute in the same room as our friend releasing wind he would indubitably vomit. The man thinks releasing wind amusing – unlike Mops, who functions by spontaneous combustion. It is his one really able accomplishment. To take his mind off sewerage I took Krantz out to gather mushrooms – needless to say, we didn't find any, but Krantz viewed the bull rather enviously. On the other hand, I have seen the bull view our friend rather wistfully on occasions. They have much in common. They take about the same size in collars but there is no question that if the bull could release wind like our friend he would certainly be able to spend more than fifteen seconds with a cow. It is interesting to speculate on how long he takes with

_____

[4] The Tiller Girls were a troupe of dancers

his wife. I should think that one good blast of wind would do the trick.

Life on the farm becomes more like Stella Gibbons[5] every moment. Six geese have just disappeared into my batman's tent to reappear again in rather a hurry. Obviously my batman believes in the motto, 'Once shat on, twice shy'. Certainly there is never a dull moment.

I must close this before I get any more interruptions but I'll write again soon. You are never very far out of reach.

Your very devoted,

G

ৎঌৎঌ

London, NW8

August 21st, 1944

Very beloved G,

There is a raid on at present which is a bit distracting for letter-writing as the old man made me promise to go underground if anything seems to be coming our way. We can hear the danger signal given in the barracks which gives plenty of time for taking cover, but they don't seem to have got together about when to let it off and it seems to sound at the most improbable moments. Unfortunately, our furniture is too modern and comfortably appreciated to allow for fat Mrs Gault to take refuge under the sofa, which would be infinitely warmer than returning to the coal hole! I believe the raids are infinitely lighter over London now, as they are shooting

---

[5] Author of *Cold Comfort Farm*, a raucous take-off of rural life

down an enormous proportion of the brutes and certainly I find them infinitely less alarming than the blitz. There is none of that grinding round and round overhead (another agitated whistling in the barracks – ah, it's the all clear this time!) of aeroplanes night after night and somehow the very impersonality of the doodles makes them less terrifying; they come and go like a thunder bolt and the only horror is the sickening thought that each bang means destruction for someone. As far as one can see they have not caused any vast destruction except for patched windows in most houses.

I notice you still incline towards the decayed seediness, like Graham Greene, when you are visualising the future. Either you see yourself as an unemployed commercial traveller pinching the bottoms of the slimmer nippies or as an unmarried remittance man whose friends won't tell you that the secret is Odol. You have always been an extremely desirable young bachelor, but after the war (where willy-nilly we have learned a hell of a lot about living), you will have additional qualifications for the post of husband that any girl would queue up for. Magin has something very attractive[1] put in cold storage for you, which she is guarding most zealously, but I hope you will take your time in choosing, as it's worth waiting to get it right.

Leslie told me the exciting news that Morar is now unbanned and we are hoping to go there for his leave in September. I am planning to return to Rothbury some day next week. It will be very pleasant to see that there Mole again and hear his strident call for 'Mi-mami.'

I wonder so much where you are and what you are doing. You must be sad to leave your obstetric orchard and I hope you are sheltering under a tree equally pleasant and peaceful!

Bless you, my darling brother, and take enormous care of

---

[1]See postscript

yourself. It looks as though the champagne corks will soon be flying!

Your extremely loving sister,

D

❦

September 15th, 1944

Very darling G,

I am sitting at the desk with a cigarette in one hand and a pen in the other but otherwise devoid of any epistolary aid in the form of an idea in my head (I am now even devoid of the writing desk as Mops has claimed it!).

Somehow writing at a desk does give you support in your intention to get something on paper, with fewer distractions than a wobbling pad placed precariously on the knees. Having filled my pen I look the part, as I am covered in ink. To return to our onions, the question is, do I now sign my name with a row of crosses denoting warm affection or struggle to wring some episode out of the past week which could possibly be of interest? Each day has come and passed exactly identical to each other. I have not even read anything beyond Hazel's book,[1] which is superbly funny and completely puts her at the top of the tree – characterisation, dialogue, situation, are all brilliantly done with here and there a peep at her capacity for writing descriptions of the countryside with a very fresh eye and delightful and effortless

---

[1] Successor to the memoirs of her time in the Land Army

way of telling you so that the reader can feel and smell it, too. I think it is miles ahead of *Green Hands*.

The day begins usually before 6.30 a.m. with Mole. The rest of the day is spent also in Mole's company so the horizon is limited even if there is no bar to activity. By the time I have got him into bed, done his washing and cleaned his shoes I feel very much in need of a cocktail but as that urge is still-born, I go down to supper and drink a delicious glass of cold water and consume a large amount of rather stale brown bread and marg. After supper, Nell does a striptease and sits semi-nude in front of one of Mops' numerous electrical gadgets. This seems to stir up all her latent theories on diseases and we hear what the nurse said (but most exactly!) to Mr Gilmour as Aunt Nell lay stretched out on the table – Mops tries to drown it with the wireless but Nell is nothing if not determined. I listen to the news, try to scratch off a letter to my old man and at 9.45 p.m. the ritual of potting Mole takes place. This done, I creep into bed fumbling about furiously in deepest gloom as the light gives him ideas that a party is on. I lie tensely still with itching nose yet not daring even to feel for a hanky, waiting and praying for him to go to sleep so that I can stretch my cramped limbs and toss about at will. He usually sits up about 1.30 a.m. wanting a 'gink' (drink) and occasionally enlivens our night by being sick (after experimenting with some of the more poisonous berries in the garden).

As you can see, life does not lack incident but lacks anything in the shape of inspiration for letter writing.

As you know, there is no-one can be ruder than our Mops when she puts her mind to it. I have seen a good many victims wriggle on the pin and have borne in grim silence a pretty strong barrage myself. It suddenly occurred to me that I could point out that these tactics were not very soothing among a household of women who were all inclined to bite back (or if politics dictated, to bite someone else instead). I took a firm grip and made my attack. Mops was quite astounded and obviously thought I was going the way of poor Aunt Jessie,[2] so my fight for suffering humanity fizzled out in abject failure. Pops told me that Grandpa Reid was the rudest man he had ever met, which interested me.

A week today I shall be on my way to Morar (although I can't believe it can ever really happen). I meet Gaga Mole at 5.45 a.m. in Glasgow and we then entrain to Fort William. We will stay for a week and then come back here for a few days and I am hoping to take Simon back to London.

Mole is now voluble in a variety of dialects but chiefly cockney and Tyneside with a smattering of Irish. He drops all his aitches. He has also begun the embarrassing habit of holding out his arms to everything male over the age of ten and calling them Daddy. I never realised that the urge for making appropriate mechanical noises began quite so young. He loves me to take him down to the station and to watch the trains, and is always pretending to be one, or a moty, or c-r-r (aeroplane). Now I realise why most men hide the shape of their mouth with a droopy moustache. Incidentally, I am delighted to hear that old Wogger has got rid of his. It was a very fine affair but too reminiscent of 1940 to be enjoyed.

I've got a very slight suspicion that the stud may be studding but I won't 'count my chickens' in case it proves to be a 'red herring'. Actually, I am horrorstruck at the prospect, and my maternal duty is of no comfort by comparison with all the ghastly disadvantages. If I can throw this off and the war within a year, I shall sit back and never do a stroke of work again. My whole being calls out for endless rich and luxurious indolence. (The result will no doubt be a glass of cold water again!)

This (like all my letters) has been written in snatches and is

---

[2] Pops' second sister

utterly puerile, but it will do my humble best to show you that I try to deserve your lovely letters when they come.

I am so longing to hear all your news and you must have had the most incredible experiences which I must be patient about hearing. I was talking to a local sergeant this afternoon in charge of the P.O.W. camp, who was wearing the African Star[3]. He was a bit of a philosopher and very interesting about his job and the war generally. It made me homesick for you even talking to him!

I will try to write again soon. I am growing so very impatient to see you again. We are having the flat all cleaned up in anticipation for your arrival!

Bless you, darling, and all my love from your extremely fond and loving sister,

D

☙❧

London, NW8

October 23rd, 1944

Very darling G,

I think of you shudderingly sitting in your cold wet truck during this pestilential weather where, even with the supposed comforts of civilisation surrounding one, the guts are gradually soaked out of you. Here we splash about in sodden clothes standing in queues waiting for the bus and cursing the Americans who inevitably ride in the few taxis to be run about. We have got light and some heat to return to and decent feedies but for you without any of these

---

[3] Awarded to those who had served in the desert

consolations it must be ghastly beyond words. The thought of it haunts me and I would gladly surrender some of my comforts if you could have them instead. Leslie and I sent you a leather jacket which I hope will keep out some of the climate. I hope it is what you wanted but anything longer than a waistcoat is extremely hard to get and I went from shop to shop before even finding this one. Gaga M. provided some of his military coupons of which he has a surplus. I hope it will arrive soon and safely!

As you will see, I am back in London again and it is heaven to be in one's own home again. The raids are so slight now we are planning to bring Mole back. If they begin to be bad I shall have to take him away again, but we can't live away indefinitely and I am longing to get him under control! I had arranged to return tomorrow and fetch him back at the beginning of November but Den seems to think she can bring him down herself, so it is uncertain whether I shall go north again or not.

I am trying to engage a maternity nurse of less nightmarish dimensions than Aunt Mary. The Puffin[1] is due to arrive about May 27th and I want to do it at home again.

Puffin wrote a little poem this morning whose sentiments I think we all will appreciate.

> 'Puffin says I like to sit
> Puffin says and think a bit.'

I remember Mole's literary beginnings were of a more virile and less meditative nature! If Puffin is a boy, we shall call him Adam, but what shall it be if it is a girl?

I was terribly pleased to get your letter 11. And I can well imagine how ghastly life must be. It seems monstrous that they should not begin leave now that the war seems to have

---

[1] Puffin was subsequently christened Jonathan

settled down again. The only comfort seems to be in the thought of what Germany will have to endure in the way of raids during the coming winter and the effect of Russia advancing into Germany on the East as we attack from the West. It can't be an alluring prospect for them.

I should be miserable if I thought you felt you couldn't write to me if you were depressed, as I write to you in all my vile moods and completely unexpurgated. It seems to me that when you are parted from someone the essential function of writing is to communicate the essence of the writer and not purely as a literary piece of entertainment. I don't suppose it is much comfort to you, in fact it may merely be an added irritation, when your lot is considerably worse than most, but I don't think I know anyone who is not eaten up with depression and a feeling of mental and physical weariness. Like any climb, when the end is in sight, the last lap seems almost unendurable. Earlier on one's mind can be occupied with other thoughts to distract your attention but, at the end, when you are tired and aching to be home one's mind can only visualise the joys of an armchair before the fire and that blissful state of peace after struggle. Your mind goes round and round on the same theme and even though you know there is not much more to bear one begins to doubt if the end can ever be reached. It will come and a year hence we will look back on it all and marvel that we were able to stick it. However hellish life may be after it can never be as bad as this! I am thankful to feel that during these months of futility and suspense I can create something permanent but I don't look forward to the next few months and my only way to keep calm about it is to make my mind jump ahead to next summer when surely the war must end and my personal difficulties will be forgotten.

I do miss you, my darling. Somehow you seem to belong here with all my other happy memories. I think of you a year ago coming home and all the agony of excitement and joy.

Our shyness when first we met, the utter bliss of having you again, yet always the restraining fingers tightening about one's heart knowing that it was not yet the end, that it was a moment to snatch at greedily, always knowing that pain lay ahead. Pray God that you will be back again soon and this time for always.

Here as I write, stretched on the sofa before the fire, while Leslie clips away in the garden, all my love and prayers stretch out to reach you. In the quietness of this room you seem so near. May my longing and love bring you some warmth and comfort so that you can share with me the quiet love and content of this moment and keep it close to you in the days to come.

Your very devoted sister,

D

P.S. The jacket is a premature Christmas present!

Capt. G.A. Watson
522 Coy R.A.S.C. (Inf. Bde.)
B.L.A.[1]

November 2nd, 1944

D darling,

You should see me now. I'm sitting snug and cosy, my cheeks glowing with rude health, my bottie basking in the heat. I am, of course, wearing the Mole-skin and it is utter heaven. If I had studiously sat down and designed a fleecy waistcoat to all my requirements, this would have been the result. I am appalled to think of what you must have paid for it but it will be my most prized, well-worn useful garment and however cold the winter, now I shall always be warm. Thank you so very much, Major Mole, Mrs Mole and Baby Mole. I just love it – and you. It is, of course, the envy of the Mess. Krantz, in particular, cannot keep his eyes off it. As if its receipt wasn't sufficient excitement for a week, I received your lovely letter twelve by the same post.

You ask about my billet. Well, it is owned by a couple who have two small boys. It struck me as being a big house for their class, possessing two sitting-rooms, a kitchen, four bed-rooms. As I find, however, that every family round here has 12 children – s'fact – I suppose once this couple get going they'll need all the space available (it is a Roman Catholic community and there are not eggs without chickens). I sleep in one of the sitting-rooms in which I have erected my camp bed. You can imagine it: velveteen sofa, ormolu clock, picture of the Pope, dresser with the family heir-looms, etc. It is quite adequate for my purpose and not quite so 'class' as Cambridge rooms but of the same type. Five of my staff sleep

---

[1] British Liberation Army

upstairs and have, of course, made themselves friends of the family with whom they sit playing cards, singing, sharing their rations, and teaching each other Dutch and English, every night. They are as happy as sand-boys. I don't see much of the family as I feed in the Mess but they are a kind couple. The children round here are a menace. They try to get at the ammunition, take it to pieces and set fire to the components. I don't mind them blowing themselves up, but I don't want them to do it on my ammunition. My issuers smack their bottoms but it only adds a bit of zest to the operation. Our Mess in the Vicarage is very posh. The vicar is a little Mussolini and thinks the English are to be discouraged and, wherever possible, preaches that the people mustn't associate with us. The people are scared of him and frightened of excommunication. Last night he turned two of his flock out of the Mess who Tom had asked in for a late drink. He pulled the old chestnut about the English being Angles not Angels – it is the same pun in Dutch. In the early days he used to come in and knock back our gin but now we are browned off with him and he doesn't get any gin, so relations are strained. However, it is a very nice Mess.

Re childbirth. I think the Mother feels for the child in a different way to the Father and generally gets more happiness directly from the child than does the Father. This, I think, is the compensation, but I wouldn't know.

I liked your crack about bints – nasal and temperamental. Had I been fulminating again about slackers? I don't remember but it's really time you stopped me. As editors say, 'This correspondence is now closed', because you must be very bored with the subject.

I hate to hear about these new rocket bombs. What is the opinion in London about Hitler's other secret weapons? Did you read the other day how he said, *re* one weapon he proposed ending the war with, 'May God forgive me for the last week of the war.' Hope it's just the ravings of a neurotic.

I see some lunatic has written a book on seeing a play 250 times in succession. I imagine I feel at the moment rather like he did after the last performance. One lives in billets which tend to create the illusion of civilisation but there are none of the normal ingredients otherwise. It is impossible to go to the town to shop – there are no shops. There are no cinemas, except the occasional army show. There are, in fact, no distractions other than those one finds oneself. One has lashings of time each day and yet not the will to fill it. Reading after a little becomes a bore, letter-writing is hindered by having nothing to write about. One has friends in to dinner but the discussion is always the same. In fact one gets up in the morning knowing that the day will be essentially the same as the last and wondering how the devil to fill it. It is like living in a vacuum. Personally, I find this period of the war easily the hardest to endure of the whole five years – which was to be expected. Sometimes I can't help wondering if it will ever be over. People talked so glibly about Christmas. Now they are talking equally easily about summer. Of course, we have made amazing progress, still that is small comfort. It is a very general feeling. I've no doubt we are better off than the Germans.

Your very devoted,

G

The jacket is heaven!!!

❧

During the course of the war I wrote a number of articles which were published in the Spectator *under a pseudonym. They were personal reflections on various matters bearing on the theatre of war in which I was currently serving. The most contentious article appeared in November 1944. It was subsequently republished in a pamphlet together with a selection of the substantial number of letters which arose from it and which aroused howls of rage and shouts of support in about equal proportions. Fifty years later it does not say much for my powers of analysis about the future and there is much in it which I now see was painfully overblown. Nevertheless, on re-reading it I would argue that it captured some of the flavour of disillusionment which prevailed in the army at the time and which would also explain a little why Mr. Churchill suffered such an unexpected defeat in the forthcoming general election.*

THE SOLDIER SAYS
By CAPTAIN, B.L.A.

The B.L.A. is well served with daily newspapers. Instead of reading, too long after to be interested, about the event in which one has participated – our experience when in the Middle East – one now reads of it when it is still fresh in mind. Do not imagine this is an altogether unqualified advantage.

Too often of late, in leader and dispatch, the soldier in the field has had brought home to him with brutal clarity the gulf that widens between his point of view and that of the citizen in England. Too often he is represented as holding opinions which he never has held, and never will. It would appear to be as true of this war as of the last that the citizens at home – even acute observers like Mr. Harold Nicolson – are totally unable to span the gap that separates them from the combatant forces.

Although any generalisation is dangerous, it is less perilous to dogmatise about the Army than about other

186

organisations. Regimentation, shared experiences, shared opinions, are all apt to tend towards a uniformity of outlook and expression. This is not to say, of course, that you will not find every shade of opinion in every unit of the Army; almost any generalisation can be demolished by reference to the particular. But there is, I believe, an easily discernible trend of opinion in the Army to-day. If I attempt to give it expression it is with the knowledge of how inevitably I must lay myself open to attack, but in the belief that the man on the spot is perhaps more qualified to write of these things than the man in Fleet Street. I speak of the Army as a whole, because as a result of spending fifty per cent of my service in the ranks I would say that officers and men largely share the same views on broad issues. The difference, if any, lies in the fact that, whereas the officer leans to the left, the man bends over to the left.

Here, then, is how I suggest the soldier of the 2nd Army is facing the world today.

(1) He believes we shall lose the peace and precipitate another war in ten or twenty years' time. He believes the Englishman is fundamentally sentimental towards his enemy – he was himself, before he saw for himself the horrors perpetrated by the Germans in France, Belgium and Holland. Knowing that his hatred will only endure until he hears the first German baby ask him for chocolate, he wants to be saved from himself by letting Russia occupy the country and direct the peace. He profoundly distrusts what he reads about Germany in the Press, and is convinced that the bankers, bishops and barons will ensure a peace that will make the Third Great War certain.

(2) He is deeply distrustful of all civilian authority – parliamentary, municipal and industrial. A large number of men in my unit will not fill up the form for the electoral register.

They are not interested in a vote, because 'it won't do me any good.' The soldier distrusts the Tories. He distrusts the Socialists, now they have become the Tories' bedfellows. He distrusts the reforms that are brought in, either because they are too late or because they were grudgingly introduced under such pressure that he doubts whether they will ever be honourably implemented. For instance, he suspects the White Paper on Social Insurance because of the previous partial rejection of Beveridge. ('There must be a catch in it.') He questions the policy of the Government on the bombed-out (many soldiers have had their families affected and know personally how unsatisfactory the remedial measures often are); and on Italian prisoners of war (quite a big political issue out here, and one, incidentally, that confirms the suspicion that Germany also will get cotton-wool treatment).

He distrusts industrial authority. He is convinced big business is making a nice thing out of the war. He has read some ugly reports of certain English firms charged in America with trading with the enemy. He suspects that the war may be no bad thing for the firm employed on munitions during the war and on the reconstruction after it. He knows that his fortunate comrades in England are often earning as much in a week as he used to earn in a month. He believes the financier was largely the cause of this war, and is already thinking of the next.

He has read about the miners on strike and he wants the nationalisation of the mines – and other public services. He wonders how, after five years of war, he will be able to compete with the civilian for skilled jobs. He is earning relatively good money in the Army now, but he expects to earn more in 'Civvy Street.' Men of twenty-five now earning, perhaps, £250 a year (taking food and clothing into account) wonder whether they will have to return to unskilled jobs that brought them in thirty shillings a week when they were twenty, before the war.

(3) He is frantically tired of the war, but he is willing to do anything to finish it. It makes him angry when he hears that England is beginning to slacken off and think that it is all over 'bar the fighting.' He knew we should be faced with a winter campaign when all the papers were gaily screaming 'over by Christmas'. He does far more than his share, he expects the civilians to do theirs. Too often he has read of safe hotels, black markets, wire-pulling and phoney exemption. In his gloomier moments he wonders how deep the rottenness has got.

(4) He distrusts the B.B.C. and the daily Press. Frequently he reads reports of events in which he has taken part wrongly reported. Too many of the things he was told about Europe he has seen for himself were not true. He is right, then, to be distrustful about facts he cannot check.

(5) Religion scarcely touches the fringe of his life. Many have kept their faith untarnished; few, I suspect, have newly found it. There is not, I think, any reason to suppose that Army life has either increased or diminished the number of the faithful.

In short, then, the British soldier is fighting for the future of the world, and does not believe in that future. He is tough, hard, honest, intelligent, cynical, kind, soft-hearted, sentimental and completely disillusioned. He is fighting not for any ideal – although he hates his enemy and the ways of the enemy – but because he knows that Germany must be utterly defeated before he can get home to his family, his football, his beer and his fireside. He asks a lot of the future, but he doesn't expect to get any of it. He does expect a bit of fun when first he gets back home. And in the next war he expects to be in the Home Guard while his son bears the burden of the day.

That represents within my own narrow experience (may I be forgiven for speaking when others better qualified hold their peace) broadly what the British combatant forces – the salt of the earth – are thinking. It is, perhaps, encouraging that Tommy, 1944, will not be fooled by facile talk of a land fit for heroes. He wants deeds, not words. It is up to the citizens of England to see he is not disappointed.

✑✑

London, NW8

November 5th, 1944

Beloved G,

It was extremely thrilling to get your letter 13 in less than a week after your previous one – it was a heavenly letter, too!

I feel your comments on Mr. Bevin[1] v domestic service deserve a few acid remarks: I will pass some. I quite admit that as a class we have shamefully 'ground the faces of the poor' and now in this brave new world we must accept our desserts. But, personally, I love the thought that the desserts may be equally shared by both sexes. Admittedly a man, poor mug, has to work five days a week doing long hours from 10 a.m. until 5.30 p.m. with a quick hour off for lunch and an occasional coffee during the morning. That's hard, and every true woman would give the poor brute her sympathy, even while she is toiling through a twelve hour day, Saturdays and Sundays included. No, let's be honest and face it, it's a hell of a life for a man and every woman is worried, too, about that daily share – the only thing that occasionally flits through the mind of a woman, as she performs six people's jobs, is that she should be allowed to choose her job. A man can be a bus

_____

[1] Foreign Minister and a Trades' Unionist tough

190

conductor or a politician and no one objects if he leaves the choice of salvage collector to some other chap. But for a woman it is assumed that chores and drudgery are her natural birthright and all her life should be devoted to the uplifting and stimulating task of cleaning out tea leaves from the kitchen sink, washing the dirty linen of her family and sweeping out the daily accumulation of dirt about the house. Now some of us girls like that sort of thing: the sight of a dirty bath makes us breathless with pleasure, a few dirty pans stacked in the sink throws us into an ecstasy of delight, but there are some who don't, perhaps, respond with just the same fervour. I know I'm eccentric but the thought of getting up at 6.30 a.m. every morning and dealing with the children, their dirty nappies and their dirty faces, dealing with the dirty grates, the steps waiting to be scrubbed, even the fish waiting to be cleaned holds no uncontrollable thrill. Perhaps I was taught to enjoy life in a different way, which wasn't kind. Of course, I see the attraction of wiping out domestic service; so much more economical to let your wife do it instead of paying a staff to do the same jobs. I suppose women, in those mistaken times when they were taught to think, to feel, yearned after that elusive and desirable delusion of justice. Perhaps it is still this queer yearning which makes me think savagely of Mr. Bevin and his balls (if he has got any) when I am told that Mr. Bevin while wishing to expunge me and mine (referring not to balls) demands that a nurse be given to him *priority* for his grandchild so that he and his may suffer no discomfort. That's true! It's also true that Mr. Morrison[2] has a W.A.A.F. to drive him (God knows why) paid for by the state so she cannot even claim a chauffeur's privilege of giving him her notice. And he keeps her at it in a 12 hour day and at the end of the day he has himself, and his friends, driven to the Dorchester while his driver waits outside until after midnight

---

[2] Home secretary

for the unrivalled pleasure of driving Mr. Morrison home again. If I could meet Col. Blimp I would shake him by the hand and call him 'Mama's own boy'.

Anyhow, sucks-to-Mr.-Bevin, I have got someone to help me with Mole and Puffin by the simple method of finding someone who was wise enough not to register her name in Mr. Bevin's book and so is able to perform the excellent work of keeping alive the feeble flicker of life at present existing in Mrs Gault's swelling body.

Puffin is terribly pleased with your Puffin hum and sings it quietly over on two notes and slightly flat. I don't mind the music of it if the sentiments sink in well!

Bless you, very darling brother. You are always in my heart and thoughts. I bought some nectarines in brandy for your first dinner home – and may it be soon.

Your devoted sister,

D

ᘓᘔ

Capt. G.A. Watson,
522 Coy R.A.S.C.(Inf. Bde.)
B.L.A.

December 5th, 1944

Darlingest D,

I am not in an entirely ideal situation for writing letters. Although, at the moment, I am alone, I keep myself alert for a precipitous entry of Madame or Monsieur when I shall have to erupt into a renewed outpouring of vile French. It is, apparently, pointless to remark that their English is infinitely better than my French, they firmly refuse on the ground that *je les moquerais.* Rather wearily I agree that if it gives them a laugh listening to me I am agreeable, but it is disconcerting when one breaks down to be prompted in fluent English. Tomorrow I am dining with them – I look forward to an evening of agony, unadulterated French! I enter and leave the house surreptitiously with a haunted expression, but seldom with success. *Mon Capitaine, vous avez bien dormi? Mon Capitaine, vous avez assez de couvertures sur le lit?* They are incredibly kind and I mustn't mock them. The daughter – 18 – is a sweet, pretty little thing, never been kissed – I think! – and is coming to London after the war for finishing. I must be careful to escape without leaving my address. So far I have progressed without interruption and the room is warm and comfortable and pleasantly furnished. It is nice to be in a good house again with a reading lamp at one's bed and running water in the basin. They have a lovely bathroom but no hot water – there has been none since the liberation. I have caused Madame consternation and amusement by arranging a bath for tomorrow by the simple expedient of getting my batman to bring some boiling water across in buckets from the baker opposite, who is allowed fuel for his business.

I got you some *Worth* which Madame says is fantastically expensive – but as it is the same price you paid in England before the war, I don't think it too bad. I shall see whether I can get it through the customs on a duty-free label. I won't send it until after the Xmas rush.

In your letter 17 – a lovely one – you are up to your old tricks of manœuvring me into a false position and then sloshing me one. You know as well as I do that I hate to see gardenias and the Embassy exchanged for essence of violets and the Assembly Rooms. I merely said that whether we liked it or not those things were happening. We are entering the age of mediocrity and greyness. It will be some time before colour is restored.

193

I am glad you liked my *Spectator* article. I had a nice letter from a Major in the War Office agreeing. I haven't seen the letters about it in the next issue yet. Pops, I think, was rather shocked. He accuses me of a liver and suggests that Xtianity will do it good. It's cheaper than a laxative, anyway. He says, 'In my case, I have had to fight pessimism all my life.' There is no doubt that he has been pretty successful in the struggle.

It is depressing to realise how life inevitably always restores a level measure in everything. If one climbs up a hill to a pinnacle of happiness it seems inevitable that some time or other one will have to descend correspondingly deeply into the pit. It is scant consolation to know that when you are in the pit there may be a hill out – 'cos it doesn't follow. You may be in the pit adjusting the balance on past happiness. However, by the law of averages, there should be a good few people due for the up-grade after this party.

All the girls out here wear Russian knee-boots which I – by no means alone – think look incredibly attractive. I have some dim recollection that appreciation of girls in high boots is supposed to be a sexual perversion – I can't think why. But why has the fashion not been adopted in England? Particularly in war-time it saves stockings and it gives a very distinctive air to the turn-out. In the case of the Watson beazles it would conceal some surplus *avoir-du-pois* on the pins.

Bless you and your nice family. I love you dearly,

Your very devoted and homesick,

G

London, NW8

December 21st, 1944

Very darling G,

I have just opened a parcel which mummy sent on to me from you with a contents of unbelievable delight. My hands are still a-tremble with sheer rapture and excitement and in these barren days (perhaps not a strictly appropriate adjective) but days without glamour or joy, such a wealth of treasure seems too much like the quality of dreams. The very names flow with the nostalgia and poetry of other times – *Dans la Nuit*, the first perfume which I ever made my own; the cream in its romantic crystal jar, a replica of a pot which you gave me on my 19th birthday which I treasured so covetously it almost went mouldy before I could bear to open it! *Je Reviens*, another milestone and another present from you – the most expensive flagon of scent I have received hidden in a tall jade box, which I still have and sniff reminiscently. The very name has a lovely promise so appropriate to the present moment, that in itself is worth everything. I wonder if a man can realise just how much a lipstick can mean, especially today, and one that is really civilised and not a stick of lip-salve thrust into a cardboard case which is all that war-time England can provide? I feel like the public speaker who says, 'My heart is very full' – but I mean it. It is so very good of you to be so generous and to be so understanding of feminine needs (both physically and spiritually!) and it makes me long to put my head against your shoulder and give you rather a damp kiss!

I have taken to my bed today with a foul cold and a glad heart. At last, I have been able to tackle some of the more urgent jobs awaiting me; no longer need I depend on safety pins to keep my underclothes in place, Leslie can face the world with his trousers securely braced which I am sure will be a relief to him, Mole will be able to emerge from his pram among the elite of Regents Park without his coat tails hanging down – the Gault family are once more sartorially impeccable. I have also to my credit eight letters, although this does not remotely cover the ground. My secretarial efforts for Simon are unending as a constant stream of parcels pour in with every post.

This may be my last chance to write to you for weeks so I shall seize it avidly but even this will be limited as Hazel rang up this morning saying she had 24 hours leave and could she spend the night here: she will arrive at any moment which will put an end to writing, I'm afraid. I received from you a superbly nauseous *carte de Noel,* which I hesitate to display on the mantelpiece among the frigidly respectable snow scenes of British gaiety. The only other which I have been dubious about showing was a witty and rather obscure drawing illustrating Gaga M. in all the glories of his hirsute nudity wearing only the rudest bum-bags, the Guards service cap, swagger cane and boots. A definite smell of *Vie Parisienne* exuding!

I have still never answered your lovely letter 16. I am very envious to know where you are, as it appears you are no longer in Holland. It sounds too gay for Belgium, but then my only acquaintance of the country was in a dank basement at the C.O.S. when I was sent to interview twenty Belgians who wanted to send Red X messages to their families. None of them could speak English, I could remember no French, none of them had the correct money and each message had to be written in triplicate. It is a painful memory!

I can't believe that the daughter of your family has remained since the advent of the British Army, as unkissed as heretofore! I am so glad they are all so kind and sweet and your letter to the parents, which I saw today, describing your progress in French made me weep with laughter. Your 1,940 francs dinner rather made my mouth water and it must be rather heaven to have a real blow-out again even at that price. I hope you let them share your bath-water from the baker occasionally!

Next Day

I am most relieved that your interest in the 'roses and raptures' of existence is still predominant. I couldn't bear you to be different. I find I am becoming madly blimp as my years increase and my horror of the continuance of this restricted and desiccated sort of living grows. So many people seem eager to sell themselves into any sort of State bondage so long as it is something different. I wish I had cut out a very amusing correspondence in the *Telegraph* incited by a complaint from 'Midland Manufacturer' on the impossibilities of running any industry under present state restrictions. This was rather regarded as an awfully caddish point of view by those obviously delighting in the extinction of M.M. in spite of depending on M.M.'s money both directly and indirectly. The final effort was a very witty and astringent contribution from 'Naval Officer'. I have a few minutes and may have a chance to add to this a bit. I have never seen so much balls as was evoked by your *Spectator* article. Winster[1] was gloriously ridiculous and it seems disastrously obvious that there are plenty of people who simply won't see what soldiers and younger people feel purely because they are frightened. They daren't admit to the mess they have made and they feel they can go on fooling the rest of the country who at last are beginning to stir to some sort of reality. We know we have got some pretty unpleasant facts to face but to be treated as a half-wit only makes me livid.

---

[1] Lord Winster wrote an angry letter, condemning the article

Later

Another few minutes, perhaps, to continue. This is a hellish way to write a letter!

Your remark about Pops' remedy for everything, Christianity, as cheaper than a laxative, was bitter but struck a chord of immediate agreement. I had just been arguing with him – a useless exercise. I said I believe that God had created a universe reaching to certain mathematical laws including the rule of cause and effect. Thus, when humans behaved in a certain way, God was as disinclined to re-adjust his rules as Euclid would be to alter his, merely to avoid an effect. I didn't quarrel with this but having accepted it as a logical state of affairs I no longer turned to God to ask him to twist the workings of the universe to oblige my particular needs, but was more inclined to do something about it myself. Pops thought this was most blasphemous and rushed to give me a large book on God. Recently I have read C.S. Lewis' *Beyond Personality* and feel that he is a man who understands the present difficulties of our age and is honest about it. His Chapter 8 onwards I felt were very sensible but I would like to ask him how one has sufficiently the urge (and not merely an intellectual desire) to give oneself over completely to Christianity. The fear of how you will face some of the more ghastly of the pits which life can hold is not enough. I am explaining this very badly but I have no time to put my thoughts into any sort of shape or there would be no time to put them down before the next interruption!

I must most grudgingly admit that the unpleasant things in life have screwed me into a slightly better shape but I am quite content to remain in poor shape and be left to wallow in my moral squalor!

I remember after the last war there was a fashion for Russian boots and hats, which we thought most alluring. The Watson pins would definitely benefit from such a mode but I suppose the acute shortage of leather and rubber makes it impractical just now.

The last time I wrote to you properly was when the Gault family were in the North. It is very nice to be back again and together. The house is crumbling fast and Ruth[2] is arranging for a horde of workmen to come and prop it up. I rather would prefer our splendid decay but Stephen is returning to England and may want to live here. I hope he won't evict us before I can land the Puffin!

Simon has settled down most contentedly and is extremely attached to the elder Mole. We have had very few alerts or rockets since we arrived, thank goodness. I seem to have been extremely occupied and yet have done nothing of interest.

Bless you, my darling one.

D

❧❧

---

[1] Ruth and Stephen Runciman, from whom the Gaults were renting their house

Capt. G.A. Watson,
10 Control Centre,
F.M.A.[1] – B.L.A.

December 29th, 1944

Darlingest D,

I am penitent, sorrowful, apologetic and any other synonym that you can think of. My last letter to you was on Dec. 5th, twenty-four days ago. I have no real excuse. True, I have changed my address but there has been – honesty compels me to admit – ample time to write. Rather has the flesh been weak. I live with Boule – Ronnie to you – Baker in the attic of a house with a roof between us and the stars, and two outside walls. The temperature without is sixteen degrees of frost. The temperature within is about eight degrees of frost. The difference is due to a Valor stove that strives impotently against superior forces. Boule and I cluster round it like workmen round a brazier and try and pretend we are keeping warm. I sit in my lovely moleskin but even so it is not letter-writing weather. Still, if I postpone any longer you will cut me off your visiting list. The Valor stove also smokes and there is a pungent smell of burnt paraffin around the room – all very jolly. However, we are probably moving to a warmer and more comfortable abode in a day or two.

Quite a lot has happened since I last wrote. I had a lovely time in my rest area – and contrary to Pops' oft-expressed fear – did not fall in love with the daughter, (the mother was much more my mark). I dined and wined well, while I had the chance. The Delbeckes had a sixty-five year old cognac which Krantz and I did justice to – and in general thoroughly enjoyed myself. The social highlight was at a dance in the

---

[1] Field Maintenance Area

Officers Mess. Krantz and I were in charge of the bar and prepared an innocent cup for the ladies. It tasted like weak claret but had the come-back of a sledge-hammer. It consisted of red wine, gin, brandy, and lemon squash. At the end when everything ran out I was making it of red wine and Guinness but the customers were still lapping it up. Altogether the sixty present – 30 mesdames, 20 officers, 10 civvy men – consumed 10 brandy, 5 whisky, 4 gin, 220 beer, 10 cordials. Fernande[2] said it was *trés chic, trés elegant.* We danced to the company band and a good time was had by all. Lucienne asked me about my friend of the bull neck. *Qu'est-ce l'officier qui fait l'échappement?* or something like that in French. I seized the dictionary and looked up *échappement.* It means exhaust pipe. Knowing his proclivity for making a noise at both ends, I asked 'Is it a double sense?' Lucienne blushed and laughed and said it was. So now you know the French for farting. She was an amusing child. I left in a flood of tears from the ladies and promises to meet again in London. Incidentally, have you received the present of toys from Fernande for Simon. If you want to write to her, send the letter to me and I will forward it. I can't give you her address. Incidentally, in the unlikely event of Simon not finding out, the toys were stuffed with sweets.

I can't say very much about my move, other than that our company, through re-organisation became two Captains surplus. I foresaw several possibilities that might have fallen to my lot. (1) Transfer to the infantry as a subaltern. (2) Staying on as a subaltern. (3) Weeks of hanging about a reinforcement unit waiting a posting and then getting a lousy one. As none of these prospects pleased, I appealed to my old Colonel and he got me posted here as 2 i/c to Boule. There are only the two of us and ten men. It is quite a pleasant, easy job. A Field Maintenance Area consists of a lot of depots for food, petrol ammunition, and so on. At the head, but not

---

[2] The Belgian family with whom I was billeted

running or administering them, is an H.Q. whose job is to co-ordinate the whole. That is our job. Actually, there is nothing in it. But I consider I am very fortunate. (a) Because there was for a number of reasons an excellent chance of getting a stinking job. (b) Because I like Boule and get on well with him in spite of his funny ways. (c) Because I keep my rank. (d) Because it is quite a good job.

I shall NOT be coming on leave in January – there was no allocation for officers in the first ballot. If, however, we get any allotment for February I stand a fifty-fifty chance, with Boule, of getting it. I shall, of course, let you know in good time in the hope you and Leslie can get leave at the same time.

The post has been absolutely chronic and has been further delayed by a new address. However, today I got your Xmas letter. Thank you very much. I quite understand that, with Mole on hand, writing is difficult.

Sorry to hear the Major is now a Captain, though I don't imagine he will lose one minute's sleep because of it. I shall stop calling him Sir now. What is his new job at the W.O.[3]?

I had quite a pleasant Xmas with Boule. We arose at 0930. Had a passable lunch with tinned turkey, pork and Xmas pudding. Retired for a little Portuguese P.T.[4] at 1400, arose at 1630 and knocked back a bottle of bubbly and retired at 2130. Probably a day of O.B.D.[5] is as good a way of passing Xmas as getting drunk and awakening with a sore head.

My principal regret at leaving the company was, of course, parting from Krantz. I would rather see him after the war than anybody I've met since I've been in the army and he was often – when things were difficult – instrumental in saving my sanity. Still, it is the way of the army to get separated from one's friends.

---

[3] War Office
[4] Portuguese Physical Training – sleep
[5] On the backs down

I owe Mole Sen. a letter and tell him that one day it will get written. Meantime, with the thought that I should be seeing you in the next month or two to buck me up I'll sign off.

As always my devoted love. Is Puffin behaving herself? Are there rockets on London?

Bless you,

Devotedly, G

❦

Capt. G.A. Watson,
10 Control Centre,
F.M.A. – B.L.A.

January 5th, 1945

My darling D,

I must make an early reply to your titanic effort, No. 18, just to hand. Although I notice that on numbers I am still level-pegging with you, on length there is no comparison.

At the moment we are at rest in a delightful little village rather like Harbottle. Boule and I are billeted with the local school-master who is rather sweet. The Belgians are without exception the most generous, kind-hearted, pleasant people I have ever met. They knock the Americans sideways. The night before last we were invited to a farm for dinner. They were simply grand – fat, jovial countrymen who were making a fabulous thing out of the black market which is used by all Belgians automatically. As they were farmers – and a very big farm at that – they had plenty to sell. We ate roast pork fried in butter, beans flavoured with a touch of garlic, fried potatoes. This was followed by roast goose, roast potatoes and apple sauce. Then apple tart, dessert and real coffee (£5 a pound) with thick whipped cream. We drank – all pre-war – sherry, burgundy, chablis, cognac. Was it good!! At the end of the evening we set off with the dignity befitting British officers and I fell flat on my back in the duck pond. It was frozen over and had two inches of water on the top. Boule laughed so much he fell over, too, flat on his back beside me and we lay there in a lake of water, soaked to the skin laughing our heads off. Next day, two large sacks of coal arrived for us. If you knew how short coal was in Belgium you'd appreciate the value of the gift. We had told them we only had a Valor stove – hence the gift. Now Boule and I sit in a blaze of heat as snug as a bug in a rug. Yesterday we were invited to tea by the schoolmaster and had three varieties of apple tart.

And then in the evening we had an incredible experience. We were asked to a farm for dinner and were received by somebody straight out of the pages of *Vogue*. Talk about *chic, élegante, soignée, distinguée,* I've never seen anything like it. She was quite lovely and very amusing. Apparently, the 'Farm' was their country house – about 400 acres of home-farming and shooting where they were living for the Xmas holidays – their town house being in Brussels. The husband – 35? – the wife 30? – and their three small children. He is a mining engineer. We ate *omelette aux champignons* (real eggs, deliciously preserved mushrooms); *porc roti au beurre à l'ail* (garlic, yes?), apple sauce and *pommes de terre frites*; and *éclairs à la crème*. The cream was about three inches thick. We drank sherry, burgundy and cognac. I trust we shall be asked back! My French, of course, is now terrific. I can understand practically ninety-five per cent at any speed, and I prattle back unselfconsciously but, no doubt, vilely. Still, I make myself understood and I speak better now with my recent practice than ever before in my life. So what do you know about that? Last night was a particularly good experience. To run into the Dorchester at Harbottle is an experience in peace-time, even. We talked – madame and I – about Chanel, and Lanvin and gardenias and horses and had a really nostalgic evening. Boule's French is a bit limited, unfortunately, but he gets along fairly well by shouting nouns at the top of his voice. E.g. *'Vin … bon … oui?'*

I had a very nice letter from John Strachey[1] about my *Spectator* article 'quite the best thing on the subject I have yet seen.' Nice of him, wasn't it? The more I see of the *Spectator*, the more I feel I shall be out of place there with its bloodless articles and its letters full of Latin tags that I don't understand.[2]

I am glad the perfume arrived safely. I will get some more if I have the chance – which at the moment I haven't – and bring it home when I come on leave. You say it will be rather agony having me on leave for such a short visit. That's surely the wrong way to look at it. Of course, I can stay out here instead if you prefer it!

Last night we had a bomber pilot spend the night with us. He baled out and his plane crashed. He had left England only a few hours before! He said he thought they were having very few rockets on London now. Is this true? They are an incredible nation. He breezed in shooting a big line but seemed genuinely touched by what we did for him including having to eat some of our execrable food. As we are such a small unit Boule and I have to have the same food as the men and it's pretty dull.

The countryside at the moment is unbelievably lovely, carpeted with thick, crisp, white snow and the sun is shining out of a cloudless, blue sky. The telegraph wires are shining white ribbons of frost. Just the day for a walk but I expect I shall stay in front of our nice fire.

---

[1] Left-wing politician who had a share-holding in *The Spectator*
[2] There had been some discussion that I might be offered a job on the staff after the war

Boule and I have decided to ask *les sociétés hautes* in for a drink tomorrow night in the hope they'll ask us back to dinner. On Sunday we are asked back to the other farm. Tonight, however, we are at present social failures as nobody has asked us out.

I'm just longing for leave to come along. I do hope you and Leslie will be able to get north. Tell Leslie he is still on my short-list for impending letters.

Bless you, my darling,

G

৯৩৩

London, NW8

January 19th, 1945

Darlingest G,

I warned you to expect a long delay between my last letter and this but I did not anticipate quite such a long stretch. However, I think the postal service will resume its more regular and untroubled way now for a bit. I have two letters of yours to answer both of which came to gladden my heart and make me laugh.

To begin with 17. I was delighted to get your snapshots and see the old familiar face without Bill Boscage. The Delbeckes[1] look very sweet and I can't think why you didn't fall for the daughter as she looks most attractive. Obviously you are going to be one of those sad cases, like Disraeli, who instead of being famous for his historic achievements becomes notable for the historic monument to whom he is married.

---

[1] The Delbeckes were the family with whom we were billeted in Belgium

206

I have been glad of the word *échappement* – a new one to me, and very useful when referring to Gaga Mole's faulty exhaust pipe.

Do you think there is anything I could buy in London which Mme Delbecke would like and is unable to buy? I would love to send her something in return for such kindness to Simon.

Your Mess dinner sounded terrific even though claret cup, made with red wine and Guinness, must be rather lowering to the morale.

Your descriptions in letter 18 of the food and drink you consumed were most unkind and made me eye the perpetual Vienna steak (or sausage meat) with which one is greeted here with even greater animosity. It was too perfect that you should end your evening in a duck-pond and I am thinking of digging one outside the front door for the joy of seeing departing guests wallow on their way out. I am sure Pops would be in a fever if you described to him your other hostess and it is rather incredible to find such *chic* in the middle of the war in the middle of the country.

It must have been extremely interesting to have a visit from the stray bomber pilot. You must admit it sounds absolutely Hitchcock –

I expect you will have heard the sad news that Simon has gone north again. We had a series of rockets one day and one fell quite near and made me panic about keeping Mole here when it was unnecessary. I miss him horribly and hated letting him go just when we were beginning to settle down here. Since he left, we have had very few rockets so we are hoping to bring him back in a week or two. I think Molly[2] would have him if it grew bad again and his nice Miss Emerson (whom we call Nan) began here and was getting on very well with him.

---

[2] Leslie's sister

Have you any idea when you will get leave? I wish I knew as it would help enormously if I could make plans. If you might come home soon, I will leave Simon at Whitewell and come north for him when you go. Leslie also might get a chance of arranging his leave for then if he had some warning. I don't suppose there is a hope of you knowing, but even a surmise might help! I don't want to leave Simon a minute longer than necessary but I would love him to be there when you are and it is not easy to take him back and forth too often! He won't add to the peace of your holiday but I think you would be amused. He knows about Puffin and because he was inclined to kick my tum if he came into bed we told him he must be gentle because Puffin was there. The other day he pointed to one bosom and said, 'Puffin there?' I said, 'Not exactly.' He pointed to the other bosom, 'Puffin there?' I said, 'No, a bit lower actually.' So he started busily to unbutton my overall to see if he could see exactly. He wanted to come into my bed but I was sitting well in the middle so he gave my tum a pat and said, 'Shove over, Puffin.' I expect you have heard he now addresses Grandpa as Angus and will have no slipping up over grace. 'G'ace, Angus', he calls if Pops seems to be forgetting. Nan was struggling to fasten his slippers so he shot off saying, 'Mummy's buncle-hook', and returned with it. His favourite expressions are, 'No sank 'oo', or, with a flashing smile 'Pees', 'Better', 'Pity, pity', 'Later', or 'More has time'. He changes so quickly he will be even more grown up when you see him.

Puffin is behaving as well as any good girl should but seems to be swelling so enormously we are beginning to anticipate quads! I could fill a bus easily by myself.

I was rather shocked to see that Edward Cooper (the entertainer) had died. One might say he had fallen in the war – he fractured his skull on the steps of a nightclub.

This is a very unamusing letter but the telephone has interrupted every five minutes and makes any sort of concentration quite impossible. I have persevered as I thought any sort of letter was better than none and perhaps soon I shall have some idle time and will be able to write to you in glorious leisure.

The news seems terrifically good and one can almost believe the end of the war might happen at any moment. I hope you are wrong in believing power politics are still rampant. I rather agree with you, except I do believe that Churchill is a big man with big ideas of being decent to the other chap and not trying to hack crumbs off for himself or for the country. If this is so, I can't see why he should be double-crossing everywhere and behaving like a complete swine. I think it is the party tradition to be utterly unscrupulous among ourselves nationally but I do believe that internationally we try, on the whole, to be decent. It seems very difficult to judge – as Shaw says, 'Who are we among so many?'

It is terribly late so I must finish this scrawl and go to bed. I haven't begun to say what I intended but I don't think there can be a chance of adding to this for some time so it must go as it is.

Good-night, my darling. I will talk to you more peacefully in bed tonight.

Very devoted,

D

✿

London, NW8

Friday, February 28th, 1945

Very beloved G,

It was lovely to see the old familiar writing today and I am
snatching at an unexpectedly peaceful moment to reply.

It was absolute heaven having you with us at Crinan and
fulfilled a longed and dreamed of hope which lost nothing in
the fulfillment. Our time after you left seemed extremely
uneventful with no further loss of hotel property.[1] We had
some wonderful days and were very sad you were not there to
share them, but we can look forward to it next time. I felt
quite transformed after my holiday in every way and have not
felt so utterly and gloriously alive for a year. Even St. John's
Wood seems full of glamour when I can see it with my mind
full of Crinan!

I am glad you had such a good time at Whitton and I know
the parents enjoyed every minute of it.

You mustn't worry about the raids on London. They are
really very minor affairs and now that I am rested I feel
completely unperturbed by them. If they become really bad,
I won't hesitate to take Simon away but I feel very strongly
about leaving at present for a lot of mixed reasons. I have a
very poor view of people who panic and jitter unnecessarily
and would be horribly ashamed to include myself in their
number. From a selfish point of view I would be much more
unhappy being separated from Leslie as I would rather be a
corpse than a widow. I resent the idea that Hitler can drive
me out of my home unless he produces something much
more alarming than he has done so far, and I have such a

[1] During a picnic a cart-horse stood on the wheel of a hotel bicycle,
thereby putting it out of action

210

deep conviction that it would be wrong to go, and such a serene and complete faith that we shall be unharmed, that to go against it would be transgressing against all that I believe in. This all sounds very pompous and stupid and so difficult to explain in a letter, but try to understand. I think everyone who can remain steadfast and normal during the war can do their part and contribute something towards the life and spirit of winning just as everyone who lets fear dominate them, not only loses something in themselves but adds to the lurking infection of fear and panic which is so close to us all these days. I can't actively do anything to help the war and I feel this is the only way I can do a bit. It was much easier in the old days when I could go out and look for incendiary bombs but it pleases me to feel that even by sitting at home with Simon and remaining totally unmoved I am not joining the ranks of the few one knows and despises who scuttle about doing damn-all, so long as they can escape the general discomfort of the war. I promise you if my nerve breaks or the raids become really bad, I will instantly admit defeat and clear out without a second's hesitation. You and I are made too much alike for you not to understand how I feel even if you do believe it's crazy!

In haste. Bless you, my darling, and all my love.

D

Capt. G.A. Watson,
S & T[1] Branch, Rear H.Q. 30 Corps,
B.L.A.

March 29th, 1945

Darlingest D,

I'm just back from a very good forty-eight hour leave in Brussels. I got in there in time for lunch and found I was staying in a very snoozly hotel, taken over for officers, where I had a vast bedroom and a nice bath-room into which I settled myself very quickly for a long soak. Then I rang up my Belgian friends from St. Martin[2] and got myself invited out to dinner. They have a perfectly charming, very modern house. We had a marvellous dinner – oysters and a *soufflé Flambert* cooked by Guylaine, such as you certainly could never buy at the Savoy before the war. Next morning, I did a bit of shopping – the prices are absolutely chronic, three coffees and brandies £2, orchids 9/- a flower and so on. Still, there is no better way of spending money than wasting it on luxuries, so what odds!

After lunch, I met Guylaine and she took me to a devastating club, furnished with sybaritic luxury, where there was a small band and a bar. You couldn't dance – only drink. The place was full of the *haut monde* and looked as if it had come straight out of a Hollywood film of 1938. I hadn't been in an atmosphere like that since before the war. We sat drinking and talking for three hours and it was extremely disturbing.

Guylaine is quite, quite lovely and very amusing. Not at all the company for a soldier! However, it was great fun and I

---

[1] Supply and Transport
[2] This was where the extravagant dinner was consumed

have never tried verbal fencing in French before. We both found it amusing. At 6.30, we joined her husband for a black market dinner before going to a French revue which was quite fun. I was able to understand it all – I think the Belgians speak more slowly than the French. After the theatre we had a drink and then went home. There is a curfew at midnight and everywhere closes at 10.00.

Next morning, I did some more window gazing – Guylaine couldn't get away in the morning. It was a very amusing, very unsettling, forty-eight hours.

Brussels is a most lovely city and scarcely touched by the war. Any one with money can live well on the black market and doesn't need to go short of anything – if they have the money, e.g. coffee is £3 a pound. As a result, the standard of clothes etc. is still pre-war among the smart set. The whole place is a bit incongruous.

Thank you for your lovely letter of March 15th (21). I was a bit surprised to see that Hazel 'will have to sleep with old Mole'. I quite appreciate that the thought behind it is in the great tradition of hospitality but commonly such an offer is made to one's friends, not relatives. Further perusal, however, convinced me that the 'old' was a term of affection and not of seniority.

The war news is incredibly good and people who should have a good idea think that another six weeks will see it through. Certainly I can see nothing now to stop us. It is quite possible, of course, that he will retire to his Bavarian joint to try and do a *Gotterdamerung*, but I don't think that is particularly important. I've seen a little of the beating he's taking and honestly it defies description. I cannot understand how the people as a whole have stood up to it without revolting. I think the end of the war may be an anti-climax. Partly because there will probably be no clear-cut line where one can say this is the end. Partly because one will probably be stuck in Germany for months – or years – waiting

213

demobilisation which in turn is probably dependent on a lengthy campaign out east.

My own remedy for Germany is quite simple. Withdraw all troops and maintain a stringent frontier patrol which would enforce total isolation, so that nothing could either come in or go out. And then let them start about clearing up the mess which will take some time. It is the easiest method of avoiding immobilising thousands of troops in occupation.

Spring is beginning in earnest. On the run down to Brussels there were a lot of trees, an absolute mass of blossom and they looked incredibly lovely. Belgium, on the whole, has not had a vast amount of destruction and some of the villages looked very clean and gay – possibly the peace is largely superficial. I went down in my Ford which made the trip very comfortable and quick.

I suppose you will be getting things organised for Puffin. When is the actual date of production? It certainly sounds pretty terrific that you have put on one and a half stone. I hope the infant won't weigh all that. It is ridiculous to talk of a falling population with all this production in process.

Give my regards to your old man and ask him when he is going to open the correspondence.

I haven't any other gossip. Write when you can. Longing to see you again, my leave seems years ago.

Bless you, darling,

Your devoted G

P.S. I'm sending you a bit of *Worth* via Mops. *Je Reviens* – sometime.

కావ్యా

May 21st, 1945

Darling D,

My thoughts and prayers are very much with you these days
– perhaps, God willing, you will already be the proud parent
of a Puffin when this reaches you. I *do* wish I had been able
to be with you. Bless you, darling.

It was lovely getting your long letter 23 which reached me
the same day as one – much shorter I am sorry to say – from
your old man. The Norfolk Rd ménage suddenly sparked
all at once.

I am interested to know that your reaction to peace was
so similar to mine. I still find it quite impossible to get all
emotional about it although at last it is beginning to filter
through to my subconscious that it is at last over. Still I am
sorry that Puffin prevented you from joining in a binge in
the West End because that would have been fun.

Here everything is fairly quiet and dull. At the moment
we are near Bremerhaven and moving shortly to a place
called Nienburg which will be our final home. It's a quite
nice little country town, about the size of Dorking. I hope
when we get settled in to start a bit of riding, swimming etc.
to pass the time. Passing the time is actually going to be the
great problem. Already there are evident signs that non-
fraternisation is not going to work. Even making allowances
for the sex-starved soldiery the German girls are extremely
attractive and they are deliberately flaunting themselves.
There is not the slightest doubt about it. They walk as near

to the camps as they can in tight, thin dresses and do a plain act of soliciting. It is asking too much of human nature to expect the troops to take no notice. Personally I see no solution – brothels would only partially alleviate the situation. They are talking of bringing a lot of A.T.S. out but I don't know that I like the suggestion implicit in this idea. I don't see why A.T.S. should be expected to provide the troops with their nooky as part of their military obligations.

I had my first bathe yesterday. Part of the lake was reserved for Germans who were disporting themselves with much noise on a beach. The rest of the lake was for the British who sat there watching the Germans from a distance through binoculars. I ask you, what can they expect?

Leave is starting again in August which means that if things go according to plan, I should get mine in October. I shall feel rather inclined to spend it in London if I can get the family down, or four days in London and seven at Rothbury. I would like to see some theatre and also make some preliminary arrangements for when I get out.

What are your plans? Are you still going to Scotland or are you going to try and get a house in or near London. If you are going to Scotland, it would be as well to winter in London first, wouldn't it?

I am excessively bored at the moment. Inevitably, I suppose one is suffering from anti-climax but I haven't really got enough to do and sitting waiting for demobilisation is a long and tiresome business. Krantz is joining us in a few days which will make a difference but even then one will be faced with the task of filling in the day. I'm simply longing to get back to civilisation and try and take up my future activities seriously. I do so want to get settled down in my house and my own job and get a wife and see some future to what I do. I expect you understand only too well.

Write to me when you have a moment. I long to see you again to talk things over with you. Writing is very second best.

Bless you,

Your very loving G

⊰⊱

POSTSCRIPT

The correspondence between Diana and I continued until and after the end of the war in Europe. But with the ending of hostilities, it lost much of its immediacy. Diana soon left London and retired to a house in the country with Leslie and their two sons. There she involved herself in a number of local activities, serving as a Justice of the Peace and as a member of the board of the local borstal. She, and Leslie, who travelled to London daily, lived in a modestly affluent style, and I and my family spent a number of enjoyable weekends under their roof, sharing the mutual interests of our growing families until we ourselves acquired a nearby weekend cottage.

In 1967, Diana died of cancer. Whilst fighting the illness over two years, she wrote a remarkable and very personal account of her battle with the disease, which was published with considerable acclaim under the title *The Journey*.

With the coming of peace in Europe, I had no choice but to remain in the army pending demobilisation. I was posted to the Head Quarters of 21 Army Group in Nienburg as a staff captain. They were debilitating days, with little to do but watch in envy as more and more friends and colleagues shed their uniforms and were demobilised. But, unexpectedly, these frustrating days were made tolerable by the arrival in the neighbourhood of Dorothy.

Dorothy was the one-time associate of my sister Hazel, who, two years previously when I was still in the desert, had written to me extolling Dorothy's considerable charms as a potential future consort. By happenstance, I was to meet her for the first time in Diana's house when I was on leave and Dorothy was passing through London on her way back to Germany where she was stationed in Bad Oeynhausen, driving a general. As Bad Oeynhausen was a town fifty miles from Nienburg, we agreed to arrange an early meeting. Some few days later, she turned up with her general and, unannounced, came over to my Mess where, as was customary for the time of day, I was playing liar dice and partially drunk on bootleg gin. I, forthwith, arranged to drive over to Bad Oeynhausen the following weekend so that we could have a picnic together.

The meeting went well and was repeated. But the entertaining of Dorothy proved difficult as, at that time, other ranks were not allowed into the few officers' clubs in the neighbourhood. As the summer progressed, this rule was modified and, with picnics in the woods and food brought in from the Mess, we managed to live a somewhat disorganised life together. Although travelling alone in a car was officially prohibited, as there were still supposed to be pockets of resistance in the all-pervading woods, I managed somehow to get over to Bad Oeynhausen two or three times a week. I optimistically and futilely travelled with a loaded revolver on the passenger seat when returning to Nienburg late at night.

So, Dorothy made my life more than tolerable in the otherwise anti-climactic days awaiting demobilisation. As my wife she has been making it more than tolerable ever since. We were married in March 1946 and have been married ever since.

Rye, October 2002